The Goddess Brigid

Her Transformative Power through the Eight Wiccan Sabbats

Russell Knowles

GREEN MAGIC

Green Magic
53 Brooks Road
Street
Somerset
BA16 0PP
England

www.greenmagicpublishing.com

Designed and typeset by K.DESIGN
Winscombe, Somerset

ISBN 9780995547865

GREEN MAGIC

For Marget & Morlaise

Contents

Section One

The Goddess Brigid, Alchemy and the Sabbats

The book you are holding is both a handbook of essentially Wiccan guided meditations (or Pathworkings – see Section Two), that are centred on the Goddess Brigid, merging her radiance with her alchemy. This is also a guide to magick and Wicca. This book is organised in two parts; in Section One that follows, you are lead straight into a series of ritual templates and guided meditational Pathworkings specifically designed for each of the Wiccan Sabbats, flowing through the Wiccan year. Through the Goddess Brigid you will find a path of wisdom, poetry, magickal integration and Goddess worship, which is the culmination of many years of dedication, ritual magick and meditations, worked and re-worked by members of the Circle of Brigid, West Lothian in Scotland. In Section Two there is a discussion on the development of this magickal practice, which serves as some rationale for the development of these rituals and meditations within our current practice as well as a commentary on Wicca from my own perspective.

I have been a practitioner of Wicca and magick for over 30 years now and, like many, I am constantly striving to improve my practice and develop my abilities. I definitely do not think I am anywhere near a point of definite wisdom, although I would say I'm the sort of older guy you see at a pub moot with an air of 'been there, done that,' kind of vibe. I think, if nothing else, the fact that I've hung around this long, have built up a fab' occult library (and actually have read most of the titles) and have actively thrown myself into many practices and trials, that I am entitled to share my thoughts and opinions on Wicca and magickal practice. (This is reflected in Section Two).

I was personally very grateful and fortunate to find a Wiccan circle operating in Aberdeenshire in the early 1990's. This was known as The Oldmeldrum Coven and was run by Marget Inglis and a High Priest who had originally been part of Gerald Gardner's Bricket Wood Coven in Hertfordshire. I will not name the latter out of respect, as he preferred to remain anonymous in life. He was very 'old-school' that way. As my friend and High Priest had preferred his anonymity in life, I choose to respect his preference even after his passing.

I served as a High Priest within the Oldmeldrum coven from 1991 until the passing of the High Priestess in 2003. Much later, after a solitary spell of magick practice where I had dabbled in

Shamanism and the odd occult order, I found the inspiration to continue the Wiccan lineage I had been party to by operating a formal practicing Wiccan circle. This was both out of respect for my High Priestess and Priest, but also as a way of giving back to the tradition that had served me very well. With my partner and some like-minded friends, we operated the first Circle of Brigid on Samhain 2012.

Why Brigid? Well initially her name kept encroaching on my mind, so I was definitely drawn to something about her. Appropriately she is a Scottish and Celtic Goddess whose name clearly harked back to original pre-Christian Goddess worship in these Isles. We, initial members of the Circle of Brigid, liked this idea of re-connecting with this 'current' of worship linking back through the mists of time to our ancestors. She is a Goddess of enlightenment and illumination. The actual root meaning of the name Brigid is related to 'elevated, high or lofty one.' Accordingly she is usually portrayed with the fire of illumination coming from her head or hands. She is the Goddess of fire and forge, a Goddess who re-kindles the light of the world at Imbolc (Spring beginning, around 1st February).

We understood that the notion of enlightenment or 'illumination' was at the core of magick. We also understood that this linking to both the forces of nature and human perfection was also a central notion of Wicca – as derived from its Gnostic roots (see Section Two). Surely there can be no more noble cause!?

Why Brigid and Alchemy? Alchemy is the art of personal transformation towards illumination and as such, the Goddess

Brigid is also very much one of its matrons. For the Wiccan priest and priestess she is both the source and the inspiration for the forces of change and ultimately self-actualisation. If you consider the first law of thermodynamics, 'energy' itself can neither be destroyed nor created. I tend to think this is a wonderful parallel for our observations in the spiritual realm also. As modern chemistry is the art and understanding of this movement, expression and change of energy between substances, then medieval spiritual alchemy encapsulates the movement or transformation of a human being from one state to another. For the self-actualising human soul, this is on an onward progression towards some idea of perfection or, to use a well-worn magickal phrase, 'Asar un-Nefer' ('myself made perfect' – Egyptian language from Crowley's *Liber Samekh*). The alchemical metallurgical analogy of inferior lead being transformed into the superior gold thus holds true. This represents the base-metal or 'animalistic' state of us and indeed our race as a species into that of more self-aware compassionate and enlightened beings.

The Goddess Brigid therefore, in her role as metal-smith transmuting ores over the fires of her kiln very much embodies this idea of transforming this one aspect to another. We at the Circle of Brigid feel that her time has come (again) for those willing to take notice and engage with this wisdom.

A major source of inspiration for us has been therefore to link the Wiccan wheel of paths of the year to the seven major operations of alchemy. To this end, we rely heavily on the work of teacher, writer and proponent of alchemy, Dennis William Hauck.

The seven major operations of alchemy are as follows:

1) Calcination,
2) Dissolution,
3) Separation,
4) Conjunction,
5) Fermentation,
6) Distillation and
7) Coagulation.

We have, we believe, quite successfully synthesised aspects of these alchemical operations together with the seasonal energies being experienced at each Sabbat! This reality of nature has been used as inspiration for the guided Pathworking at each Sabbat. We also acknowledge, very readily, that these have been inspired by Brigid herself as muse. You will also acknowledge this when you experience these Pathworkings yourself!

I suppose this is one of the aspects which drew me to Wicca and, I suspect, many others; that there is a feeling or belief that there is an inherent human-natural spiritual truth contained within, which has survived extinction despite the efforts of zealots through the ages. We therefore acknowledge these significant seasonal shifts with these eight separate actions we call the Sabbats, naturally representing mindfulness of the alchemy at these spiritual hubs of Wicca. This notion of celebration or feasting or 'festivity,' by the way, is noted among scholars to be ubiquitously observed among most or all human cultures.

Meeting and celebrating at each Sabbat can be seen as the central jewel of Wiccan practices. Certainly this cycle forms the template of the Circle of Brigid's yearly social calendar, and there is an expectation that we will meet to celebrate the key Sabbats at their appointed time. The four Greater Sabbats are the cross-quarter days which are also known as the Celtic fire festivals. The other four are known as Lesser Sabbats, and comprise of the solstices and the equinoxes. A useful summary can be found in the appendix section at the end of the book.

The Eight Wiccan Sabbats on the Wheel of the year

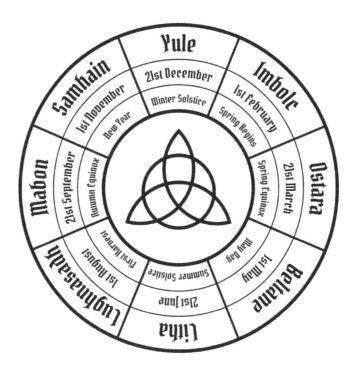

These are the 'intersect' of the seasonal shifts of our Mother Earth and the interplay of life, and death, on this planet as the sun and the light waxes and wanes. This interplay can also be felt within our own psyches and, to me, this is why Paganism is a 'no brainer' as a spiritual path in terms of connecting our lives with the planet, solar system and beyond. As I wrote, in an early kind of pamphlet, for people interested or joining the Circle in 2012, "Sabbats allow practitioners a way to consciously connect to the Earth, and subconsciously connect to the archetypal energies around and within them. We, at the Circle of Brigid, see this as a step towards some realisation of who you, the practitioner, truly are in the world."

For each Sabbat I give a brief description of the concepts to have in mind, under the heading 'to consider.' I always tried to put this at the top of any rituals which were disseminated to participants over the years as a quick and handy key for the main aspects to have in mind for any particular Sabbat. This is a reminder of what myths are involved or which forces dominate the season.

The important 'keys' to any ritual are the feelings and the mental images that should be employed throughout. I will stress, though, that absolute mastery of mental visualisation is not required for magick to work. One does not need to perform special feats of mental gymnastics or possess the ability to 'see' the Gods or elemental spirits 'in person' in a circle. The feeling of the situation is all that is required for complete success – as well as the knowledge that when a practitioner calls on the Gods and Goddesses involved, communication is taking place; despite what your own assessments of the level of your own skill or success may be. This is vital advice imparted to me by Marget Inglis – one of the wisest Wiccan High Priestesses to have helped carry the torch of the craft over the years and into the 21st century. I wish everyone could have access to such a person, though if I can do anything to impart some of her wisdom in these pages to you, then I am in some small part paying tribute to her.

Brigid Internal Power Charge. Goddess protection

Before (and after) you engage with any form of magickal work, of course it is good magickal hygiene to both protect yourself from unwanted attention and gain an element of control of whatever you will come to interact with on various other planes of existence. The following exercise is designed to create a safe interphase between you and other energies and agendas, as well as creating an intelligent 'shield' that will protect you and only allow in those powers that you want to work with, when you are 'lit up' as it were, energetically on the astral planes.

Close your eyes, relax and focus on your breathing. It should be slow and rhythmic. You should feel your body relax and be momentarily free from the stresses and worries of the day – whatever they might have been.

Focus on your image of the Goddess Brigid. Just see her in your mind, whatever your notion is, it is the best way to start.

Now, add the image of her as an Earthly power, moving through the caverns of the world, snake-like and watery. Also, she is of the heavens like star-light, bright and mysterious. She is also a Goddess of fire, golden like the sun. She moves through the air like a powerful wind that blows the boughs of mighty trees, or a wistful whisper of breeze caressing the delicate meadow flowers. All of this she is, and more. The rain, the heat, the dew and the hard crystal mineral earth.

She is the mysterious spark of life, between fire and frost, the very essence of the living universe. Call to all these places. To frost, to earth, to water, to air and to fire, call to all these places to come forth to you, the Goddess Brigid from the very material of existence itself. Say to yourself or aloud: Hear thou me! Mighty wonder of the world, my Goddess, my power, my ally to my body and soul. Hear thou me and come to me as my protector and guide.

Feel the energy move through the universe, move through the astral towards you. The Goddess as a very bright star-like energy arriving from both below and above you, from your left and right, above and below, from all directions around you, northwest, southwest and all corners and directions, like the spokes of a wheel in multiple directions; each direction now aflame with a fiery sword of protection. She fills your shadow body and magickal aura culminating in a bright shining presence in your heart.

Say these words of power:

> Cha laigh bruaill-brì orm,
> Cha laigh suan-dubh orm,
> Cha laigh druaill-drì orm,
> Cha laigh luaths-luis orm.

The essence of the goddess pulsates at your heart, the bright light casts a shadow on the wall as it shines though you, illuminating your aura – banishing all unwanted energies and purifying your aura. The swords of power flash and flame in all directions. Anything that was clinging to you without your knowledge or permission has now been removed or is evaporating under her blazing radiance. Feel this power shining within you – strengthening your own aura which becomes as strong as a suit of armour.

Her power flames around you, see the sterilising alcohol like magickal flame burn intensely around you – before settling to a gleaming mirror-like shield. Her energy from all directions continues to enflame, engulf and energise your aura until you are satisfied that it is quite full.

Ask the Goddess now – "Keep me safe and intelligently allow in only those influences which I allow and will benefit me. All unlucky or unwanted spirits be gone and sent away with your light. Only lucky spirits that do me good herein!"

Know you have a shield and the essence of the mighty Goddess of Protection within you.

Perform this at the beginning and end of each magickal practice. It would be good to remember this, so that you do not have to glance back at the book, breaking your concentration somewhat. Perform daily for good results. She also serves as a powerful protection during all spirit conjuring work.

Power, The Rune &
Transactional Magick

The *Wiccan Rune* was originally written by Doreen Valiente in 1957 and is a mantra of intent to begin any circle working. It starts with a call to the elements, then an affirmation of the tools and works of Wicca, culminating in a call to the Gods to aid in the magick. Participants usually walk in a circle building energy as they do so. However, we've always remained still, hands joined, sending the energy around us as we chant the rune, intuitively letting the chanting become faster and faster as we feel the power rise.

The following is the Circle of Brigid version of the rune. I make no apology for 'diluting' or 'corrupting' the original Valiente version. Neither do I profess this version to be in any way superior (I pay much heed and respect to the original). I relay it here as a record of the version we use and the version adapted from the one I received from Marget Inglis.

CIRCLE OF BRIGID RUNE

Darksome night and Shining Moon,
East, then South, then West then North,
Harken to the Witches Rune:
Here we come to call thee forth.

Earth and Water, Air and Fire,
Wand and Pentacle and Sword,
Work ye unto our desire,
Harken ye unto our word.

Cords and Censer, Scourge and Knife,
Powers of the Witches Blade,
Waken all ye into life,
Come ye as the Spell is made:

Queen of Nature, Earth and Moon,
Horned Hunter of the Night,
Lend your power unto our Rune,
Work our will by Magick Rite.

By all the power of Earth and Sea
By all the might of Moon and Sun
As we do will – "So mote it be,"
Chant the spell and be it done.

The energy is spiralled around from your right hand to left. When practicing this, one may see a faint bluish haze or full-on cone of power in the middle, between everyone. It does not matter what you see or even feel... It's there! This charged atmosphere can now be used to 'power' the proceeding events. {Note – the rune itself can be used as an offering towards a particular spirit entity or enterprise as an exchange or gift for healing or other services you may have need for in the circle. Therefore, if you are a solitary worker, then this will work fine for your purposes; The Circle of Brigid has used the rune as an offering of energy to great effect in other spirit operations such as Goetic magick}.

The Wiccan circle will look familiar to any student of magick, in that it comprises of a Solomaic circle, the greater rite of the Pentagram from the Golden Dawn and the Watchtowers of the Enockian system of Dr John Dee and Edward Kelly. So, given that we are petitioning the 'mighty ones', as Gardner refers to them, to come to our aid to both protect us and help create a balanced zone for magick, what is in it for them? You may argue that the Wiccan rune could be an offering of power (as stated), as are the flowers and incense. As a working magician/Shaman who works with spirits on a regular basis, I know that pacts, allies and relationships need to be maintained and nurtured. To quote a well-known Occult teacher and writer:

> *"Others, like myself, feel the Western gods, angels, and spirits have gone without feeding for far too long; thus, if you feed them as part of your magick, they respond in a big way."*
>
> **AARON LEITCH**

Therefore, we at the Circle of Brigid have invented a method to induce, promote and honour our relationship with Wicca and these elemental forces (it's about time!). The following is an add-on after the Wiccan Rune if you wish to honour the mighty ones (as I would recommend). You never know – this may be the missing link you may need to make your magick work the way you like.

Concentrating on the power say:

Queen of Nature, Earth and Moon,
Horned Hunter of the Night,
Lend your power unto our Rune,
Work our will by Magick Rite.

Then holding palms outwards towards the East and projecting the power raised as an offering to the Watchtowers of the Air, say:

Effervescent and swirling free,
Earth to air sublime ecstasy,
We welcome you unto our feast,
Accept this offering mighty allies of the East!

Again, concentrating on the power, repeat saying:

Queen of Nature, Earth and Moon,
Horned Hunter of the Night,
Lend your power unto our Rune,
Work our will by Magick Rite.

Then holding palms outwards towards the South and projecting the power raised as an offering to the Watchtowers of the Fire say:

> Incandescent light and flames,
> Air now fire – combustion reigns,
> We welcome you unto house,
> Accept this offering mighty allies of the South!

Again, concentrating on the power, repeat saying:

> Queen of Nature, Earth and Moon,
> Horned Hunter of the Night,
> Lend your power unto our Rune,
> Work our will by Magick Rite.

Then holding palms outwards towards the West and projecting the power raised as an offering to the Watchtowers of the Water say:

> Effervescent boil and froth,
> Fire to water bursting forth,
> Cool condensing moistens and wets,
> Accept this offering mighty allies of the West!

Again concentrating on the power, repeat saying:

> Queen of Nature, Earth and Moon,
> Horned Hunter of the Night,

Lend your power unto our Rune,
Work our will by Magick Rite.

Then holding palms outwards towards the North and projecting the power raised as an offering to the Watchtowers of the Earth say:

Consolidated hard as stone,
Water to Earth and blood to bone,
We welcome ye, so come ye forth,
Accept this offering mighty allies of the North!

Again, concentrating on the power repeat saying:

Queen of Nature, Earth and Moon,
Horned Hunter of the Night,
Lend your power unto our Rune,
Work our will by Magick Rite.

Then, holding palms outwards towards the Altar and projecting the power raised as an offering to the Lord and Lady, say:

Queen of Nature, Earth and Moon,
Horned Hunter of the Night,
Receive our prayers, love and boon,
We thank you with this Wiccan Rite!

Being mindful of a transactional, beneficial and two-way process of transaction will invariably improve your magickal practices. I'm grateful to Jason Miller for permission to use this quote from lesson 5.

Strategic Sorcery Correspondence Course Lesson Five: Offerings:

"If you make offerings a part of your regular practice, then you will develop more powerful and long term relationships with the spirits than simple tit for tat contracts. I have been told by one practitioner that this is one of the primary differences between the Bokor (Sorcerer for hire) and Houngan or Mambo (Priest of Priestess of Vodou) in Haiti."

The Ritual Template

'To consider' paragraph – highlighting the main aspects of the Sabbat to keep in mind.

A description of the alchemy of this Sabbat.

Template for each Sabbat Ritual:

To commence: Goddess Brigid Internal Power Charge (see page 7).

A lit candle on the alar for focus.

Power: The Rune and/or transactional magick.

Poem for use as offering of words and to call on Brigid.

A Pathworking which takes the practitioners through a journey of the Sabbat.

To end: Goddess Brigid Internal Power Charge (see page 7).

If you are in an existing coven then I can envisage you incorporating the following ritual content into your own framework of a ritual magickal Wiccan circle and working with the consciousness changing aspect of the magick. Or if you are a solitary practitioner, you can easily access the meditations and experiment with the formula of the rites expressed here.

We believe that this body of work is useful and different from any other source material currently available. These rituals can actually be used without the need for any coven or magickal paraphernalia at all. Parts of these can be simply read and felt with enough intent and belief. They are a meditation! That, we believe, is enough to create a link to the forces involved. You can also derive as much joy by merely reading and engaging with the imagery as any story you may enjoy reading to pass time, whiling away in a coffee shop, for example. Although as a caveat I would urge you to be careful – as the imagery may take your attention somewhat and leave you a little spaced, depending on your level of so-called absorption. So make sure you swig a coffee or ground yourself with a nice full-fat muffin before moving off. Enjoy the journey – Blessed be.

Imbolc

"Spring cleaning was originally a nature ritual"

DOREEN VALIENTE

To Consider: Imbolc allows us the opportunity to let go of the past and to look to the future. This is a core aspect of being human, of being conscious. Letting go of past mistakes affords us the opportunity to self-edit our long-term memories and grow appropriately.

Understanding that growth and renewal in nature occurs in cycles can be quite therapeutic. Nature herself is most adept at overcoming the odds, getting rid of the old, trimming away the dead wood and re-emerging with new vigour and potential.

The same type of sentimental feeling can be applied to the self. The Hermetic tenet 'as above so below,' is probably one of the most important magickal philosophies to be considered when working with these Sabbats. That which occurs in nature is also mirrored in the processes of the psyche and soul of a person.

Imbolc is the time to consider overcoming the old self and triumphing with a new self, emerging towards illumination. This may have been hard and involved some trials and ordeals. However, rejoice in this knowledge that old patterns can be overcome. New directions and opportunities are ahead.

Imbolc is the Sabbat associated with our Goddess Brigid. She is the force of quickening nature. The fires of her forge have purified our souls in the alchemy of 'distillation' undertaken during Yuletide. The chemical process of distillation has created a new purified mind set and soul ready to spiral round the wheel of the year once again.

The Celtic word 'Imbolc' translates as 'in the belly,' referring to lambing, the potential of life waiting to burst forth from the womb. Now the time is ripe for a new self to emerge, burned and cleansed of all the old dross. There is celebration in the air for certain. I like to think of the cycles of the year as occurring to us as a spiral. Each year we walk the spin of the wheel – but this is not in isolation; rather the journey is building on the years before as we progress through the spiral of our lives.

Imbolc Alchemy: We have chosen Imbolc, the feast of our Lady Brigid as a time representing to us the alchemy of **stage 7: coagulation**. This is the final stage of transformation. Despite being the first point chronologically to start our journey, the alchemical operation is the final, operation 7. How can this be so? This is because the wheel of the year is a never-ending cycle. We penetrate the mysteries starting at Imbolc, because we start at the end, before going around again. This will become clearer to you as you progress through the Sabbats.

Chemically speaking, coagulation can be seen as the precipitation, once again, from the purified vapour products of distillation or the actual transformation from an inferior substance to a new pure one. In other words, the gold from our base selves has been wrought at the end of this stage.

Brigid is our Lady of Shining Radiance, who represents the gold in us. Further, she has guided us to this point where we meet at the crossroads of the Sabbats between one cycle and another. The culmination of the distillation at Yule has given us that gold, that understanding of ourselves. Reflect on the previous cycle of the year that you have been through and ask yourself, 'how much have I changed since last year? In what way am I the same person? In what way am I a stronger, more illuminated soul?'

Dennis William Hauck in the *Azoth Ritual* provides us with invaluable insights into this stage/operation:

> *"In alchemical metallurgy, the baser metals are transformed into incorruptible gold during this stage."*

> *"The Product of the Conjunction is fused with the spiritual presence of Distillation. The purest essences of one's body and soul into the light of meditation."*

Connections to Imbolc are clear here. The energies of the feminine renew the world and a renewed consciousness can grow.

Our Lady of both water and fire, bring us forth anew from the boiling cauldron of her alchemy. It is the completion of the yearly cycle and new beginning.

Template for Imbolc Rite: A lit altar candle for focus. Goddess Brigid Internal Power Charge (see page 7).

Power: The Rune and/or transactional magick.

All or 4 different people: At some given point recite the words of the poem to honour and guide-in the Goddess. Three chimes (for the Triple Goddess) are given at the start to prepare the mind for the meditation (each Stanza could be given to a different person for a collaborative effect), and ended with a chime to denote a short moment of meditation as the words are contemplated. The final Stanza is followed by two chimes to make nine (a number associated with the Gods of Wicca).

Imbolc Poem/Offering of Words: Offer palms outwards towards the centre of the altar (e.g. statue, veve, symbol) which represents Brigid! Feel the power and imagery flowing towards her as praise and offerings. All say:

Mighty Goddess we both honour you and evoke you with these words:

My Lady...
A torch is lit on the horizon,
A golden sun bears a fanfare of joy for your return,
A choir of Aralim illuminates the dark skies.
We feel you in our heart, blood and soul.
Brigid's feet have touched the Earth,
Your lithe footsteps bear snowdrops in your wake.

We love you being here with us.
Energy – flooding through the gates.
Who opened this gate, opened our hearts.
Understanding gives rise to beauty, strength and mercy.
We are grateful for you, for lighting the many paths.

Power, a pregnancy free to push, expand and express its own will.
Your will has returned.
Will to live, will to experience and be at one with the Earth.
Aye, we feel him in our blood, rooted in the ancestral mind.
He of the standing stone, of forked branching gnarled bark;
He will make the very Gods and death to tremble before him!

And she, this Lady brings the light.
With her we shall live, a mote minute and dance a moment in
the sun.
Praise for the torch she brings; praise her in her mighty name;
Brigid – Of the fire and light!

Everyone: Meditate and see/feel the image of the Lady Brigid arriving/invited into the space.

All say: Great Goddess Brigid – lead us peacefully through this Imbolc Pathworking.

Imbolc Pathworking: Retire to a sitting or comfortable position with feet on the floor. Relax the body.

Become aware of the ground where your feet are. This is connected to the reality all around us, the cool damp earth of the forests and the landscapes beyond the confines of the temple crackling with life stirring. As you sink into a peaceful meditative state you consider the image of the Goddess Brigid as a fire Goddess – offering her fire from the palm of her hand out to you. You know that you are at a beginning point in the cycle with her, though you also know inside that you have met at the crossroads of time like this on many previous occasions.

Her voice enters your mind, accompanied with a feeling of real security, bliss and spiritual love, a spiritual love that soothes you to the core. In that instant, you realise that despite all trials and ordeals that occur in life, at the end of times, everything will be alright. Her voice startles your mind:

"Every step we make together builds the gold within you!"

Your consciousness awakes and you see in your mind's eye, the image of an eye in a triangle, blink and then focus on you. As it does so, you feel the energy of the spiritual world merging with this one; lifting and vibrating the energies in the room or circle around you. You watch in awe as you are aware of her energy as she casts her spell of beauty and fertility over the land.

You understand the lessons from previous journeys on the wheel of life that you (as a witch) can take part and interact with the mysteries around you. Reaching out you feel the energy from our divine mother arrive at the soles of your feet as a pulsating blue orb.

As you petition the Goddess for aid, the power pulses and travels upwards through your body. Feel the pulsing under the arch of your feet and the sense of swirling bluish light travelling through your body and aura until it arrives at your heart.

As the blue energy pulsates there, feel your awareness go into the heart chakra, or qabalistic sphere of Tiphareth – experience how this feels.

As you are experiencing the images of this heart centre, suddenly from your mind's eye she appears bright and beautiful and terrifying all at the same time. For a moment a Celtic fiery Goddess spirit and then older; a force of nature incomprehensible, benevolent and all powerful. She fires your soul with the red ochre flame of illumination. This is almost overwhelming; however you know she will take care of you. You let this fill your senses as the energy – now pulsating with the love of the Goddess, resonates there.

At this moment again reach deep within yourself – feel your own energies pulsating and merging with the energy of nature – right in the belly – of Imbolc. Let the Green Man stir within you also. 'The fire that lights the green fuse' renewing you.

At this point you realise just how much connecting with these natural forces has changed you. You are aware of a bright golden sunrise and as you watch it a shard of energy speeds towards you on the flaming arm of the Goddess. The fire in her hands penetrates your heart chakra with a flood of energising fiery golden power merging with the cool blue pulsing from the Earth. As the power surges through you again you sense the image of the eye in the triangle, though this time it contains something more than an incomprehensible or remote image of an eye. This time there is a sense that an aspect of your own soul is regarding the physical and mental sense of you. Brigid's guiding voice rings clear in your mind;

"The eternal bornless point of nature meets at the crossroads of time with the ever changing dynamic universe, yoked together they bring blessedness. This cross I hold and give to thee is a symbol of both the cycle of change and perfection."

Ask yourself, how have you changed since last Imbolc? How would you like to change again?

Understanding this, you call to Brigid;

"Radiant Goddess Brigid – please deepen my realisation!"

You know that you have been heard and that the effect is now duly manifesting as you have willed. She smiles and takes your hand and you feel yourself lifting out of your body. Your spirit is like a vapour evaporating into the atmosphere, rising on the spiral of Kundalini which snakes Earth-Goddess-like through your energy system and above and beyond you.

You have the sensation of floating above the clouds, high above the earth. You glimpse the swirling void in the place of some spiritual truth. You know this is a place beyond the normal confines of the astral planes that interact with dreams and the earth. Suddenly you feel alone but at peace in the infinite expanse of reality. You feel confident that you have earned the right to exist here. The power of Imbolc, the seeds of change and the illumination you have gained from working with this mighty Goddess through the cycle of the seasons have empowered you like never before. This, you sense, is an Angelic realm, where perfection and peace are the orders of being. You bask in that feeling of peace, a feeling of completion and satisfaction. However, you are now aware of another presence that is not of the Goddess Brigid, but feels just as benevolent with extreme feelings of love and empathy for your existence. You turn your gaze towards the source of the feeling and find yourself rushing towards what looks like a garden of flowers and life existing in summer perfection.

It is quiet and still as the air is filled with many butterflies and small multi-coloured points of life, which, you muse, must be fairy-like entities enjoying the peace and sunshine. The very sun itself seems larger and brighter, to your mind like some alien star on an alien world, more golden and radiant, yet you do not have to squint or shield your eyes. You walk among the large flowers, feeling a bit like Alice in Wonderland. Some of the flowers you recognise, such as honeysuckle, wafting in the breeze, their pink flowers illuminated and seeming to stretch out in the light air to drink in the golden light. Other flowers amaze you and make you gasp, huge bright azure and bluish round flower heads blaze and dominate the scene as you turn a corner to be confronted by their being. You hear the sound of peacocks cawing and you see one strut casually on a lawn, its huge array of feathers catching the sunlight, throwing off a dazzling rainbow hue of colours.

Already you know that you want to stay here forever to rest and enjoy the fruits of your labours. This is a place that even a Goddess would remain, stay and talk with you in person. As you wonder about this, you feel a little emotional; as you know that you are visiting and will have to leave at some point, though you are happy to experience all you can for the time being. Presently you walk into a circular clearing where statues of various Goddesses and Gods adorn the lawn, some with water flowing from their hand, others with fire and others with incense billowing from softly swinging burners. Many others are adorned with woody vines and flowers. As you take in the scene you begin to wonder how old this place is when you realise that someone is sitting on a small stone semi-circular stool several feet to your left. They are either reading something or weaving or doing something with their hands, quite relaxed and happy. Instantly you recognise this person, and only you can tell if they are old or young or male or female. However the recognition jolts your heart as you recognise this is like the best friend you ever had. A memory comes to you of a dream you had once when you were very young, of this person coming to visit you and comfort you when you were ill. You are sure it is the same person and you run to her/him and hug him/her with all your love. When you do, you feel integrated and whole and the universe makes sense for the first time in your life.

"I am your very soul" the person says, "how great is it that we meet like this!"

The soul is bubbly with laughter and filled with happiness. You are now also aware of the Goddess walking around the circle, tending to the statues, pruning here and there and looking after the elements expressed by each one. You think to yourself,

'How mighty is she, who can work with each element in turn!?'

You want to run over to her and hug her also, to finally be at one with the Gods, though you do not, knowing instead that she is already a part of you. Her voice speaks in the peacefulness of the garden;

"Your consciousness has achieved great things to be blessed with the image of your eternal power here. And there is another…"

You realise that to your right hand side there is another being and you almost do not want to turn to look, such is the feeling of power and awe that it exudes. You know instantly that this is an angel, powerful and frightening to behold. It is your guardian angel who is also a guide in your existence. You turn towards the being that is happy to receive you there. What the angel says to you now is for you alone. Here now you hear the message: You must meditate here on a sense of a message you would receive from your own Holy Guardian Angel (HGA).

You understand that at each turn of the cycle, that as many steps you take to work towards your HGA then it will take the same towards you. Suddenly, as you are overwhelmed with the experience again the guiding hand of our Lady gently takes your hand and leads you through the wonders of the garden. You know your soul is within you, integrated with yourself and that other beings here have nothing but empathy and love for you. Some you see as you walk through the garden with our Lady, smiling faces adorned with the golden sun. Some you faintly recognise as they have come to see you here and wish you well. The flowers smell like incense and the summer air begins to chime with a distant clock somewhere in the vast heavenly space. The Goddess places her arm around you and you praise her as you slip into a peaceful and restful state. You know it is time to return, though you care not. You are not sad as this feeling of change and perfection makes you want to come back to earth and enjoy this knowledge.

The chimes now will gently chime eleven times and within this time you will return to the circle or physical plane where you started. You feel yourself peacefully flowing downwards, as if becoming denser, like vapour condensing slowly back towards the earth plane. Each chime feels like the dew of yourself and soul becoming denser liquid and the then solidifying back to the physical body. After all the chimes, when you are ready – look upon the altar candle and gather yourself back to waking consciousness.

Now enjoy the feast of Imbolc with the company of Gods and ground yourself.

Goddess Brigid Internal Power Charge (see page 7).

Ostara

"The dark and the light in succession,
The opposites each unto each,
Shown forth as a God and a Goddess:
Of this our ancestors teach"

DOREEN VALIENTE (*Witchcraft for Tomorrow*)

To Consider: Ostara represents one of the perfect points of balance on the journey through the Celtic Wheel of the Year. It is the Spring Equinox, where night and day are of equal length. This is also attributed to balance of masculine and feminine, yin and yang, conscious and unconscious as well as inner and outer balance.

Here the seasons are now waxing, where light will 'defeat' the dark. The natural world is gaining momentum with life and vigour. Principally the sun is growing in strength and the days are becoming longer and warmer. The full promise of Imbolc has burst through with the splendour of fertility on the Earth at Ostara. Remember Brigid is also a Solar Goddess, so it can be considered that her fire is burning brighter and brighter, flooding your soul with blinding illumination.

The energy is expansive and irrepressible. It is the first day of Spring! The Goddess Ostara is also honoured to celebrate fertility and re-birth!

Ostara Alchemy: Our alchemical journey continues as purification continues. At this exciting time of beginnings and rebirth, I have chosen to associate this Sabbat with the alchemical operation 1: Calcination. The soul has a sincere desire to ascend and reject parts of ourselves that no longer serve us. Repressed energies can now be transformed and flow anew, to reinvigorate us and give us the energy needed for action, to fulfil the hopes and will started at Imbolc.

With our everyday life, this can be experienced as the bliss of being freely and actively engaged in creative acts.

The body's energy channels align, recharge and elevate every fibre of our being.

Dennis William Hauck in the *Azoth Ritual* provides us with invaluable insights into this stage/operation:

> "The first operation of Calcination, which works with the element Fire to burn away dross and reveal hidden essences. The word "Calcination" (and such related words as "calcify" and "calcium") are from the Latin root calx, which means limestone or bone. To calcinate something is to burn it until it turns chalky white, reduce it to ashes, or cremate it."

This would be a good time to take up regular Kundalini exercises (such as Sahaja Kundalini meditations – see references).

Template for Ostara Rite:
A lit candle on the altar for focus.
Goddess Brigid Internal Power Charge (see page 7).

Power: The Rune and/or transactional magick.

One, all or four different people: At some given point recite the words of the poem to honour and guide in the Goddess. Three chimes (for the triple Goddess) are given at the start to prepare the mind for the meditation. Each stanza could be given to a different priest or priestess for a collaborative effect. The final stanza is followed by two chimes to make five and then further balanced by the four chimes to follow in the rite = nine!

Ostara Poem/Offering of words:

Offer palms outwards towards the centre of the altar (e.g. statue, veve, symbol) which represents Brigid! Feel the power and imagery flowing towards her as praise and offerings.

All say: Mighty Goddess we both honour you and evoke you with these words.

Carefree Goddess of pulsing lust, expanding joy.
Whose magick creates the world anew, like a bright new morning.
Walk among us in this sacred space unto you our Lady!
To you, to you, to you.

Man of Earth and Life, we sense your open eye,
behold your priests and priestesses!
Celebrating your kindling flame of power and merging with you
willingly.
We gather in honour and gratitude for you Lord of life.
(As it is our will to walk and grow a-right with thee).

Whose magick force that through the green fuse drives the
flower.
A point of divine potential ever exploding into her expanding
infinite rapture.
Let this growth symbolise this day.

Let their mighty allies be our allies also.
Let it be your right and let it be my right, to be at one with the
Earth;
Expanding, pushing life!
Let it be our right to grow unhindered as it is theirs, and no
other shall say nay.

Renew coils, renew skin, the black-red viper means us no harm.
Radiant bright one, rekindles the very Sun.

A battle cry bursts the early morning mist – Wake up!

Feel the warmth on your face at last!

Love is the Law!

All: Great Goddess Brigid – lead us peacefully through this Ostara Pathworking.

Ostara Pathworking: Place your hands, palms flat on any solid object around you. Take a few minutes and tune into the slight pulse, the living energy circulating both through you and the Earth herself. Think about the spiritual energies in and around you, flowing freely. Allow these energies to begin filling your body, replenishing your shadow body/astral body with power. This is the shadow power known to sorcerers of old, you let it empower your life-force and all layers of your soul and self. Now ready, the power quivers inside you, you feel like a swallow on the line, ready to take flight and follow your instincts.

Feel your shadow self slightly rock within you, to and fro, one and two – with each breath. As your breath slows you relax and now your astral body flies at high speed, barrelling over the ground like a supersonic jet as life blurs around you. You enjoy the experience; there is nothing to fear and nothing to experience but joy.

You find yourself standing quietly in an expanse of grasses and wind-swept tufts of bog plants as the cool air laps around you, which you find both cold but comforting at the same time. This is evidently a place that has not changed very much in hundreds of years of human existence, perhaps since the retreat of the last great age of ice over ten thousand years ago. You can tell you are standing alone in a remote highland glen, perhaps an earlier circle of Brigid met there many centuries before.

As you stand there in the glen, cool, misty and quiet, you feel sleepy, not even half awake. But just as you are accepting that this is a cold and relatively barren place, suddenly her light beams into you with all the force and vigour of a bright morning shard of light, blinding you into confusion, forcing you awake. Although you should have been expecting her, the glare and suddenness of this light caressing distant stones and illuminating the entire glen around you is both dazzling and surprising in the extreme. For an instant, you understand what to be 'awake' actually means as your brain makes connections at lightning speed and more of reality is revealed to you.

As you contemplate this, the very wind softly whispers in your ear;

"Have you the courage to know knowing, the sense to see real seeing?"

You look, with some small sense of dread, as two beings move in serpentine waves towards you, over the old historic landscape; a nightmare from tribal memory, perhaps!

Although your mind is bright and awake, you are frustrated as your body is lethargic and incapable of putting into action what your spirit is willing you to do, as the entities rise up in front of you. Two fiery but elegant looking snakes apparently made of molten rock, spiral before you; each fixing you with an eye that burns into your brain. They understand your frustration; they can feel it emanating from you. Take a few seconds to look at them, marvel at the sight of them spiralling before you, weaving around each other, spiritual heat radiating from their glowing bodies.

A voice, sweet and cool as the Earth itself, speaks into your mind. You recognise her as an aspect of the mighty Earth Goddess Brigid of the Glens and you trust her implicitly:

"Dare you accept the knowledge of yourself?"

Wholeheartedly, you embrace the opportunity, despite the fear in your heart of the raw power of these beings. Opening your arms in a T-shape posture you fall towards them. You feel yourself falling, falling, and falling far into the Earth itself, Deep into the very bosom of our Lady. Two great porcelain arms, like temple columns, catch you as you fall and lower you into a great cavernous hall. Red lights flicker and dance up the rocky sides and glint off marvellous stalagmites jutting meters into the air here and there. The snakes spiralling around the columns are providing some of the light as they coil and twist below your body on the two arm-like columns you now rest on. You both feel and see them, like ribbons of blood and metal, twisting and plunging over each other like a massive DNA double helix, driven by some unimaginable, inexhaustible source of power.

You sense, for a moment, the might of what appears to be a magnificent living 'machine' churning with raw 'star-like' power somewhere in the depths beneath you.

You look upwards, trying to glimpse the radiant face of Brigid but instead all you can behold is a white hot flame, emanating peace. As you stare, you realise now that her arms have embraced you and the twisting snake like spirals of power on her arms are now twisting along your arms from the elbow to each hand. Looking at your hands, you see that each palm of your hand is pulsing and glowing.

You think about Ostara as a time of growth and renewal; of equilibrium and balance; of finding who you truly are and doing your will on Earth and growing towards that will, that outcome. Much as the seeds have their will to grow and complete their lives also.

As you look at your hands and petition the Goddess for aid in your life, you lift your hands to your temples. The power is instantly transferred to your Ajna Chakra, the third eye. An image of an eye in a triangle flickers before you.

At this moment, you ask Brigid for aid in this endeavour. If you have a project or anything else you require help with at this point, ask now...

As you send out your thoughts, you begin to feel three presences move around – walking purposely, singing to themselves an old Celtic song – maybe even a pre-Celtic language, to focus their work.

The words are about life, about working towards a purpose while honouring the elements all around.

You see glimpses of tools and the instruments of smith work. Three they are; weavers of fate and servitors of life, powers with access to the very churning white-hot machine mass at the centre of the universe below you. Molten metal spills before and around you, showering you with noise and white hot sparks of heat. Although you relax, there is no burning or pain, only a pleasant feeling of relief as the three fates expertly peel away parts of your aura and being and toss these into the creative fires far below. Steam hisses up from the white-hot void as old parts of you are recycled in the cauldron of fire within the belly of the world.

Layers of your ego are peeled away slowly and carefully as you sense old negative thoughts that you have been holding onto; (just as they have been holding onto your being) evaporate and dwindle. You glimpse an old wise woman's face lit by a coiling rod of what looks like white hot metal. She winks at you, working with skill and focus as she pulls the soft superheated substance, like a metal snake, with large forceps into a coil of power. You feel another hand feed the powerful new parts back into and around your aura and body.

You have the experience of your own soul staring out from behind your eyelids, observing everything dispassionately. You remember this presence of your soul, which you encountered at the garden at Imbolc and you smile at the recollection of this being. This is a peculiar sensation and for a moment you are scared that you will forever remain like this; a soul looking out of the window of your eyes. However, a sensation of calm envelopes you and your perception gradually returns to a more comfortable and stable form, while your mind, body and soul feel integrated, invigorated and refreshed. The power of the Earth moves through you as never before and you rejoice in the smell of the green glen and warm air swirling around you.

Eventually the clangs of the smithy work fade and the visions of the beings around you disappear. You awake on a mattress of lush smelling grasses as birds sing nearby and insects pleasantly buzz around the small flower heads. They seem to have just awoken, the same as you have. You sit up and look around at the ancient landscape, now feeling a part of it more than ever; made of the same stuff, forged in the same fire, blessed by the same kiss of life. Although you cannot see any aspects of our Lady, you know she has not gone away, for this is her time, her arrival on Earth is more powerful now. You stand as before, in the old glen but with renewed consciousness you feel it pulsing and feel happy with this knowledge that others do not see. The power behind the curtain has been shown to you and you are blessed and privileged. You feel more solid and psychically renewed for whatever journey lies ahead. You thank her mighty Brigid, Goddess of Light, Life and Liberty.

Eventually you hear a distant drum beating, echoing over the glen. As you listen to it you are gently transported back to the temple of your own space on the physical plane where you started and, when you feel ready, look upon the altar candle. Use this focus to gather all parts of yourself back.

(Drum or chime or both beat softly in nine repetitions of nine regular strokes)

Goddess Brigid Internal Power Charge (see page 7).

Beltane

"Forests spreading, peace returning,
Where the Pagan fires are burning,
Now the inner light discerning,
Let the sleeper awake!"

DOREEN VALIENTE

To Consider: Beltane derives from the name of a God Bel (or Bil) and the Old Irish word 'tene' meaning fire, so literally this Sabbat translates as 'the fires of Bel'.

This Sabbat is a feast marking the end of the darkness endured in winter and celebrating the coming of the light again in summer. This is also a time where life was observed to return to the Earth. So the ancients understood well that light equals life. In terms of the solar masculine aspects, the Sun God has returned to the Earth and continues to grow in his strength. His light reflects and empowers the Goddess. In turn she nourishes him. I think there has been some confusion in pagan circles in terms of which God or Goddess represents Sun, Earth or Moon. Brigid for example is a triple Goddess associated with the moon – but also has solar or fire elements. I think they can best be thought of as intertwining and interplaying energies combining to make all flourish with abundance. To quote the mother of modern witchcraft once again:

> *"All the Gods are one God and all the Goddesses are one Goddess, and there is one initiator. The one initiator is one's own high self, with which the personality becomes more and more integrated as the path of spiritual evolution is followed."*
>
> **DOREEN VALIENTE** [Witchcraft for Tomorrow]

Beltane Alchemy: For this Sabbat, it is fitting to consider an association with the energies of operation number 2: Dissolution. In the laboratory, dissolution equates to dissolving the inorganic ashes left by stage 1 – Calcination back into solution. Again, Dennis William Hauck in the *Azoth Ritual* provides us with invaluable insights into this stage/operation:

> *"Psychologically, Dissolution represents a further breaking down of the artificial structures of the psyche by total immersion in the unconscious, the rejected part of our consciousness."*

> *"Within the alchemist, the dissolving Water of Dissolution can take the form of dreams, voices, visions, and strange feelings which reveal a less ordered and less rational world existing simultaneously with our everyday life. During Dissolution, the*

conscious mind lets go of control to allow the surfacing of buried material and tied up energy. Dissolution is the continuance of the kundalini experience. Dissolution can be experienced as "flow," the bliss of being well-used and actively engaged in creative acts without personal hang-ups or established hierarchy getting in the way."

Beltane Ritual Template

Lit altar candle for focus.

Goddess Brigid Internal Power Charge (see page 7).

Power: The Rune and/or transactional magick.

One, all or 4 people: at some given point, recite the words of the poem to honour and guide in the Goddess. Three chimes (for the triple Goddess) are given at the start to prepare the mind for the meditation. Each stanza could be given to a different person for a collaborative effect. The final stanza is followed by two chimes to make nine.

Beltane Poem/Offering of words: Offer palms outwards towards the centre of the altar (e.g. statue, veve, symbol) which represents Brigid! Feel the power and imagery flowing towards her as praise and offerings.

All: Mighty Goddess we both honour you and evoke you with these words:

As wild winds blow, the furrow's cast,
The frost it yields to warmth at last.
And life it shakes a dusty coat
& barks and calls and clears its throat.

The cats stretch out upon the grass,
buds and leaves unfurl from masts.
Wind and Sun and Water and Earth,
Conjoin together, then give birth.

The coil is sprung, the race is seen,
full-tilt across the village green,
behind closed doors the witches' rites
or in the woods come Beltane night.

To stir the Gods, and magick will,
To tap ancestral currents still
And breathe it in and radiate.
Illuminate and celebrate.

All: Great Goddess Brigid – lead us peacefully through this Beltane Pathworking.

Beltane Pathworking: As you relax, allow yourself to become less attentive to the physical surrounding. Close your eyes and tune into 'other' energies in the room. You sense fleeting movements within the stillness of the room. You know there are energies fluxing and concentrating within the circle. The mechanisms of magick are primed listening, awaiting the signs to carry out your will through time and space. Some of the energies you have created are here while others are external, drawn to the place of magick by our act of will.

Energy is a gateway by which we peer through the veil. Still there is more, the ancestral current of others before us have made the well-worn path we call Wicca. It extends to Oldmeldrum and beyond, branching like a gigantic tree across time and space, linking every single brother and sister, priest and priestess. Its roots do not stop at Dafo, Gardner and Valiente – but echo at every sacred landscape, old symbols on old church walls, Green Man and Shiela-Na-Gig, forgotten caverns and further and further back to the mighty titans at the beginning of time. You thank the Lord and Lady for putting you here, now, at this moment with these friends and this knowledge.

As you reach out to the Gods, through the spiralling mists, through the astral, by stem and shoot and leaf and bud, by root and branch and stone and rock, you are transported to a forest where you behold the image of this mighty tree – with all its connections to every Wiccan and pagan on the planet. A vast white elm, glimmering, majestic and bright; growing fuller and fuller, brighter and brighter in the universe. Stars span the skies far ahead. You see that you are but a small light on a small branch, but essential nonetheless to the overall shape of the tree. Now, as you step back further, you see that there are even other trees glowing in the forest of humanity. We celebrate the forces that both define our humanity and help guide it through the chaos of changing times.

You feel filled with love and appreciation for all fellow humans, animals and plants as you walk through a forest of tall and old trees. This is an ancient place. The path snaking through is old and worn and you wonder about the various priests and priestesses, Wiccans, Witches, Druids, Shamans and Vodouisants who have walked through here before you. As you walk, you begin to hear voices sing, carried through the foliage, echoing and re-bounding off trees and stumps from you know not where. Carefully, as you listen you can make out the words of the Wiccan Rune. The words convey a feeling of nostalgia and knowing to you and you are both excited and curious as to who is performing this Rune, deep in this magickal place. As you walk, the sounds become a little louder and more audible. There is a short silence followed by a ringing sound as you hear the words spoken:

> *"I was born at the dark midnight of the year and as the year grew, so did I. God of the greenwood am I, mighty hunter, wild and free. But now the tides of summer are starting to flow, when the Sun dances. As the Sun waxes, so shall I. The sacred night of Beltane is come again. The woods and meadows flower forth. Let us rekindle the balefire!"*

You smile to yourself as you understand that, while you do not see the people performing this; their voices can be heard here in the magickal wood – as their offering and celebration of the Gods and spirits of this season. You shout to them, "Yes! The Gods can hear you!" And just as you shout this you understand that by hearing this and knowing this, the Gods have granted you the power to benefit from the people before you, by those who have made the path easier to follow for each new generation of Wiccans, for each soul going around the Wheel of Life again.

As the balefire is lit, the forest glows from all directions in a warm orange light, like a morning sunrise, giving warmth and comfort everywhere. You realise that this powerful light cannot come from one ritual fire as it is everywhere at once. This light, you now realise with awe and wonder, emanates from a being far different and far older than human beings. It is the light of the Goddess Brigid as she moves purposely through the Earth. You are lucky enough to see her for an instant. A smiling benevolent face radiates fleeting through the trees and foliage spreading warm and illumination. She is wearing a long flowing garment made of transparent threads of fire and gold, which move in slow motion like a dream. Her feet do not seem to touch the ground as she glides effortlessly through the forest. You wonder if the voices create her or call her into being. Was she ever there and the wise ones before us just connected with her? That is the mystery that our linear minds are as yet ill equipped to answer.

As she moves through the forest the light dims but does not fade. You try to catch her but you cannot keep up as she does not use the paths we make – travelling as she does in ways and dimensions we cannot see. You almost feel like giving up, when you hear the sound of running water not too far away.

You follow the sound, which becomes louder and more rushing at every turn until you glimpse, through the trees, reflected light from translucent globes of water scattering from rocks here and there. Walking towards them, you come into a clearing where a huge rock face, glistening with clear spring water, towers above you. Looking up, you see the source of the spring covered with ferns and large pretty flowers in full bloom, as if celebrating the source of our mother's life-giving force gushing forth.

The water flows freely down the rock face pooling on the earth, tumbling over stones and earth in one long glistening river of light, going where it wants, expressing itself with upmost honesty and freedom. The water looks so cool and refreshing. Realising that this is a sacred spring, you eagerly drink from it, longing to taste the refreshing water and to gain its spiritual fortification.

The magickal water permeates through you, flowing through your body, dissolving as it does the purest essence of you. Soon your consciousness expands as it, and your body now infused with the water, becomes as water, fluid and free. You observe the strange phenomena of all your parts separating yet remaining as part of a jostling continuum, flowing easily where they are meant to go. Understand this feeling of allowing yourself to flow exactly as you are meant to, unhindered by obstacles or challenges in your life path. You understand the lesson of water in this state – obstacles and pools along your journey, in fact; provide you with character and individuality on your path towards your future.

Your body now coalesces back towards a solid form, as you move snake-like through a calm pool of water, aiming for the other bank.

As the serpentine motion is felt along your body, you are aware that internally the same motion is pulsing energy through your energy system. This is the energy of the Earth, dragon power – the motion which gives birth to possibility.

You take a moment to feel a kinship with the power as it moves freely through you.

You emerge from the water in this pool. Water cascades into the pool from a waterfall on the opposite bank. You realise that this is where you entered the pool from the forest above.

You are filled with an overpowering sense of peace in this place. This is yet another gift from our Lady Brigid. Now that you have found this place – it can be ever yours to return to, to relax and safely ponder the spirit realm.

Sitting quietly on the bank, you make contact with your lower or genital chakra. You feel it pulse with renewed energy; the experience of Dissolution in the bubbling stream has cleansed your aura and given you clarity of thought. An understanding comes to you – 'why am I waiting for the Gods to tell me what to do at this moment, what do I really need?' Reaching out to the Goddess you try to communicate your feelings about why you are here. You say:

"Brigid – please give me the true knowledge of myself!"

The energies respond both around you and within you. Your consciousness expands and you marvel at the clarity of the warm water, the dappled light reflecting here and there through the water. You see the fire of the sun in the water and know that all elements are perhaps not as separate and polar opposite as you thought. You thank the Lady for this spectacular insight. Perhaps other truths about you come to the fore as clearly as the waters themselves.

As you sit and reflect on the forces around you and of the ancestors who walked through this place you feel complete calm and inner peace.

You can take this inner peace, knowledge and calm with you back to the physical place you are in now. The chimes will ring nine times and you will collect yourself calmly back into the room during this time. And when you are ready, focus on the altar candle to ensure you are fully back to waking consciousness and ensure that all parts of your mind are back to our time and space. To end: Goddess Brigid Internal Power Charge (see page 7).

Litha

"Everything around you is spiritual, and everything around you is energy. This is the Law of Energy."

ANASSA ROSE

(Eighth Law of Ten from 10 Most Important Laws for Successful Magick)

To consider: A major solar/fire festival of summer where the Sun is at the height of its power. This is a moment to consider a sense of perfection and completion. This is the longest day and there is celebration of life and plenty. Though even now the seeds of Yin are ready to swing back from this height of Yang, like a pendulum. Bees work to pollinate the flowers and we can work to ensure our future plans. Being mindful of the presence and nature of the elemental forces are key here also. These are the allies and 'old friends' of the Witch throughout every circle and magickal working.

Litha Alchemy: I have chosen to associate the alchemy of Litha with that of operation number 3: Separation. This means exactly what it says on the tin; the solution we gained after dissolving the calcination products or ashes is now filtered. Unwanted dregs are discarded and instead we further nurture the purity we have gained so far. Dennis William Hauck in the *Azoth Ritual* provides us with invaluable insights into this stage/operation:

> *"Much of this shadowy material is things we are ashamed of or were taught to hide away by our parents, churches, and schooling. Separation is letting go of the self-inflicted restraints to our true nature, so we can shine through.*
>
> *The process of Separation retrieves the frozen energy released from the breaking down of habits and crystallized thoughts (assumptions, beliefs, and prejudices) and hardened feelings (emotional blockages, neuroses, and phobias). This misspent energy is now available to drive our spiritual transformation."*

Litha Ritual Template

Lit altar candle for focus.

Goddess Brigid Internal Power Charge (see page 7).

Power: The Rune and/or transactional magick.

One, all or four different people: Recite the words of the poem to honour and guide in the Goddess. Three chimes (for the triple Goddess) are given at the start to prepare the mind for the meditation. Each stanza could be given to a different person for a collaborative effect. The final stanza is followed by two to equal nine.

Litha poem/Offering of words: Offer palms outwards towards the centre of the altar (e.g. statue, veve, symbol) which represents Brigid! Feel the power and imagery flowing towards her as praise and offerings.

All: Mighty Goddess we both honour you and evoke you with these words;

> As this morning broke, the sky exploded into light.
> Our souls respond, our fibres pulled by unseen might.
> These forces lift our spirit and warm our face,
> and root us both in time and space.
>
> The winds of nature blow up a storm,
> the Etz Hayim shakes us to the bone.
> For those that feel this warmth caressing,
> have Brigid's favour, the Lord and Lady's blessing.
>
> The tree its branches flex and sprout,
> the tarot spins, and lives play out.
> For those that 'see' wisdom will come,
> light never fades, we are the Sun!

On this day we know this rite.

As our ancestors stood on Litha night.

To all good Fairie, Gods and holy ones we salute you still.

Love is the law, love under will.

ETZ HAYIM, *Qabalistic Tree of Life*

All: Great Goddess Brigid – lead us peacefully through this Litha Pathworking.

Litha Pathworking: We find ourselves standing in honour of the bright sun on a beach at high noon. The water of the mighty ocean gently laps around your feet. It is quite warm water but cooling in comparison to the hot sand. As you stand feeling the warmth beat down a memory from the last Sabbat reaches your thoughts. Surely if I desire to know myself as I have stated, then I learned that I have to meet the Goddess half-way. You have heard and read this notion a hundred times – in order to make myself fit for spiritual transformation first I must make my body and mind as a temple.

Remembering the last time you meditated by a pool, you decide to continue to link with the power of the season and the tides of change, like a sailing ship you wish to harness these to your own transformation. Placing your fist over your heart chakra and applying a little bit of pressure you say:

"I am spirit! I am pure awareness!"

You feel a real sense of achievement having done this and the Sun grows stronger, warming your chest and face. You are not sure if it is the Sun or the pulsing radiant energy of the heart chakra radiating forth, sending you into a feeling of absolute bliss.

You are wondering what to do next as you look around you. The white sand is endless and carved into pleasing ripples by wind and wave. The breeze on your face, carrying the sound of the surf to your ears makes you feel alive and happy to be standing unhindered and allowed to be at this time. Some birds trace a path through the air, as if magickally not bound by gravity. You watch them effortlessly wheel and dive overhead, stealing the silence with their alien-screeching. You recognise these as a tropical species and their presence adds to your happiness. The slow rhythmic beating of the surf compels you to relax further as time seems to slow almost to a comforting stillness. Then as you turn your head to watch the green energetic birds jostle from view you see an inscription on a piece of driftwood erected there by some earlier visitor to these shores. It reads:

"The first essential is the dedication of all that one is and all that one has to the Great Work, without reservation of any sort. This must be kept constantly in mind; the way to do this is to practice Liber Resh Vel Helios...The important thing is not to forget.."

(words from **CROWLEY'S** *Magick Without Tears* – pages 6 and 7)

Eagerly you decide to make a start, like the fool in the tarot you are filled with potential and promise as you make identification with the noon day Sun high above you. You place a fist over your heart chakra again and feel that chakra point pulsing and becoming more energised in response. Guiding this sensation with the mind, you say these words from *Liber Resh Vel Helios* (see references):

> *"Hail unto Thee who art Ahathoor in Thy triumphing, even unto Thee who art Ahathoor in Thy beauty, who travellest over the heavens in thy bark at the Mid-course of the Sun. Tahuti standeth in His splendour at the prow, and Ra-Hoor abideth at the helm. Hail unto Thee from the Abodes of Morning!"*

You wait for the thunderous rush of power or the feeling of becoming one with the solar power. You are met with silence. The breeze continues to pleasantly caress your face but you feel despondent and annoyed. Doubts creep into your mind, 'what am I doing?' Could I be wasting my time?

Strangely, you watch yourself move away across the sand, walking, hands in pockets with a dejected gait back along the shore. You watch as this form of you slumps down and stare nonchalantly into the horizon. Simultaneously though, you also watch yourself remaining still, eyes closed facing the radiant horizon.

You realise that you are neither of these characters and that you have become spirit – pure awareness, aware of either possibility.

The standing version of you speaks:

> *"Spirits of Litha come to my aid – so mote it be!"*

You now see tall strong blinding astral beings surround your standing form ready to lend their energy towards you. Looking down upon you they lend their energy, their fire to you, strengthening you, healing you and giving you the energy for all you wish to achieve this year.

However, your other form does not hear this nor see the mighty benevolent beings do their work. Instead they surround this form of you doing nothing and they wait.

You think in spirit – 'if only I knew what to do..?'

The Sun you noticed has moved a little and a vibrant red hue spreads over the horizon. You look towards the large luminous orb of the sun again and think to see a silhouette of a person or people walking in your direction.

As they near you see the form of yourself who had walked away in doubt and slumped into the sand. Although this time garbed in a fine red robe with symbols representing the Sun and Brigid's cross decorate the robe. This other self is being led by a woman who radiates beauty and kindness. She has a sense of knowing and power you have never felt in another human being. You know in your heart, without asking, that this is an aspect of the mighty Goddess Brigid; although she now appears to you as just any other person, dressed in white summer garments, and jewels. Tattoos on her arms of snake like shapes and symbols make her appear like any bohemian traveller on an island holiday you might pass on the beach. The other form of you walks back towards the standing form, hand in hand with the guiding hand of the Goddess, walking now with more confidence, as if changed by initiation. She occasionally whispers in the ear of the robed figure.

She talks to you now in plain language; almost as an old friend or an equal. Her soft subtle Scottish lilt conveys history and many past lives. She says:

"You will know better now, the bright warm Sun is ever in our heart, young love."

You find yourself back in the tau shaped standing figure; however you also find that you are wearing the robe that was on the other version of you. You understand that both aspects have been combined. Although you are not in spirit you know that somewhere Brigid is close to you guiding you but you cannot physically see her anymore.

You are still feeling happy and alive, the feeling of presence surrounds you, although you see nothing, you know what is happening as the image of the tall fire beings of light working their magick on you is still fresh in your mind.

However, now you have an inspiration to do something a little different and you return radiantly towards them. You understand that Brigid is telling you something in spirit – you are the little Sun, these beings look to you for comfort.

You have come to understand that to give is just as powerful as receiving in spirit. You now stand in this place and radiate heat, love and light to all beings in the universe. Just how many you touch is a measure of just how bright you become.

It has been a long lesson, but still the sky is blue, for this is the longest day and there is plenty of time.

You place your hand on your heart chakra and thank Brigid for her patience and guidance. Eventually you hear the distant chiming in the circle and, taking your time, slowly leave the sound of the surf and return to the circle of Brigid. The chimes will ring nine times and you will collect yourself calmly back into the room during this time. And when you are ready, focus on the altar candle to ensure you are fully back to waking consciousness and that all parts of your mind are back to our time and space.

Goddess Brigid Internal Power Charge (see page 7).

Lammas

"Hoof and horn, Hoof and horn
All that dies shall be reborn
Fire and rain, Fire and rain
All that dies shall live again."

IAN CORRIGAN (other verses attributed to Z. Budapest)

To Consider: Lammas or Lughnasadh is a festival of feast for Lugh, the Celtic Sun God of light. We understand that at this time of year, the Sun (God) has transferred his power into the grain, which has ripened in the fields. This power is harvested as we cut down the bodies of the crop. If you think of the time honoured image of death carrying a scythe, then similarly the crop is sacrificed and scythed down. This idea of sacrifice to ensure that life goes on is quite embedded in our psychology.

The power is then harvested and made into the first new bread of the season. Again we see in nature this notion of energy transduction, of alchemy, as 'the one thing' is transformed by an act of will or magick into another. The perfect analogy for the alchemically minded Wiccan then is to understand that we humans make the labour and preparation, but nature has the power to change and charge what is necessary. The power moves through the land, to the crop and to the bread. The sacrifice is an illusion; the life-force is the thing that is sustained. The harvest provides the sustenance for yet more labour and renewing of the process.

Lammas is a festival which focuses on seeing the desires you may have had at the start of the year begin to unfold and become physical reality.

Lammas Alchemy: Operation **number 4 Conjunction begins**. This is the first real operation which looks to unite the practitioner with energies which transcend the material or matter realm to that of spirit.

Chemically speaking, conjunction is the recombination of our existing solution with some kind of catalyst or chemically reactive substance to force a change of state or an amalgamation with new materials. So the notion of sacrifice and changing state is very appropriate at Lammas. Again Dennis William Hauck in the *Azoth Ritual* provides us with invaluable insights into this stage/operation:

> *"Conjunction is really a turning point from working with the first three operations below (in matter) and working with the last three operations above (in spirit)."*

Lammas Ritual Template.

Lit altar candle for focus.

Goddess Brigid Internal Power Charge (see page 7).

Power: The Rune and/or transactional magick.

One, all or fur different people: At some given point recite the words of the poem to honour and guide in the Goddess. Three chimes (for the triple Goddess) are given at the start to prepare the mind for the meditation. Each stanza could be given to a different person for a collaborative effect. The final stanza is followed by two to equal nine.

Lammas Poem/Offering of words: Offer palms outwards towards the centre of the altar (e.g. statue, veve, symbol) which represents Brigid! Feel the power and imagery flowing towards her as praise and offerings.

All: Mighty Goddess we both honour you and evoke you with these words.

Mother corn sways and bends in waves in unison.
The breath of life revealed to naked eye,
Solemnly treading over the fields and hedges.
Buzzing summer air sweeps heavenly over the grasses,
Sown with love, furrowed with will.

Quietness stills the land.

He does not weep as voices yell from the old wood;
'There's blood upon the corn!'
Though a stalked body is no a corpse,
But a harvest for the miracle of nature's communion.
The bread and blood are theirs to give.

[H.P. raises the chalice of ale]
Praise Demeter, Praise Ceres, Praise Lugh.
Hail to the one thing for the few!

All: Great Goddess Brigid – lead us peacefully through this Lammas Pathworking.

Lammas Pathworking: As you relax in the circle you begin to reach out to the energies of the season. We start with the very air itself. Now you send your astral self into the realms of the east, whose gateways we opened and whose energies were availed to us from our mighty allies in the realm of the element of air. In the realm of the sylphs you feel the air blowing nonchalantly over the fields. You sense the trees whisper the names of the old Gods across the forests. The breath of life weaves and stamps its patterns across the landscape. In this fluid state the template of the alchemy of the season is seen. Ever changing, ever flowing, a dynamic dance of life in never ending whirls and rushes. The sound of the wind whooshing through the world is loud and unstoppable. You see in this moment that the element of air is not separate but a moment in the evolution of the unanimous 'one thing' of alchemy.

Your mind is filled with energy and your thoughts run clearer. The very air has a secret 'intelligence'. Your soul has glimpsed this in the circle before and now you fully see the reality of this. You now consciously know what you have intuitively felt – that this intelligence is looking back at you while you observe this wonderful fluidic and dynamic realm. Take a moment to feel the power there and any impressions you may have of this place.

You sense the long slender beings we call sylphs move around you. You watch them cradle seeds blown in the wind as they show you how they both respect and nurture the living natural world around us. As you look at their forms dancing and wheeling in the wind, like birds at play, sunlight glints off their bodies and the energy is absorbed by the atmosphere. As you travel in the breeze with them you watch the leaves rattling and the trees swaying below you, the voice of the Goddess reaches your mind:

> *"Behold the breath of my body which sails in the wind. That which flows through my hair and bellows through my garments is the soul nourisher of the world. There are no other Gods where I am, I the night sky and the impossible heights. Blessed are you my priestesses and priests who receive the breath of my kisses upon your radiant brows."*

A shiver runs up your spine as the words fill you with ecstasy and bliss. The warm summer air blows freely and ripples over a large field of barley. You drop out of the breeze you were travelling within and watch as it whisks across the field like ripples on a pond. You have felt like you wanted to remain in that state for longer, such was the bliss of the expanding flying realm of air. You feel the fresh breath of life permeate your aura and fill you with a powerful light sky blue energy. It feels endless and captures the feeling of now and forever, like the dream of a summer's day. You salute the air elementals like old friends and bless them this Lammas as they continue to thread their magick over the world.

You now return to the sitting position within the circle. You take a few seconds to collect yourself before the journey continues.

Now that you have returned to the solidity of the circle we now focus on the South. This time you send your astral self into the realms of the south, whose gateways we opened and whose energies were availed to us from our mighty allies in the realm of the element of fire.

This realm is very comfortable and warm; you feel an almost inexhaustible sense of energy and heat. Again you have a sensation of movement, of spiritual beings, the salamanders carrying the will of this realm. Once again you sense an intelligence and life force behind this aspect of reality, which watches you with keenness and interest. You have no fear. As a Wiccan these are your allies, the powerful forces of nature that you have worked with many times in the past. You have a sense of these beings being quite empowered at this time of the year. Amazingly you are overlooking the same landscape as before, though now see the myriad of shapes and forms bouncing around like the inside of a kaleidoscope sending light and heat everywhere. The Sun is not in one place, but everywhere you look. This image is hard for you to comprehend but you accept that at some level you are witnessing the fractal nature of reality and the ability of the Sun to penetrate and permeate all levels of being. As you are wondering about the Sun God, of myths of Lugh and Bel you hear the words of the Goddess booming around you:

> *"I am the secret flame of your heart and the giver of life. The golden flame of the evening Sun is but the auburn echo of my long flowing locks of hair. My radiance uplifts thee but for many, too much to behold am I. The warmth on the world is my passion, which stirs in the cauldron of my reception. Though the God matches my love, I alone burn in joy and beauty for all, for all time. There are no other Gods where I am. Blessed are you my priestesses and priests who receive the warmth of my love for all your life and being."*

You feel the warmth of the Sun and the energy of Lammas flow through your body and aura. The light and energy flow everywhere, seeping into all parts. You see the myriad of flashing forms absorbing onto the grain, swelling them on the stalks to full capacity. You notice that much of it has also absorbed into you – a free gift just by visiting this realm. You realise how much of an ally the light of the south has become to you as you thank them as old friends and depart back to the solidity of the circle. You have felt like you wanted to remain there, in the warmth, like on holiday on a summer's day, though you know you have more to see and do.

You now return to the sitting position within the circle. You take a few seconds to collect yourself before the journey continues.

Now that you have returned to the solidity of the circle we now focus on the west. This time you send your astral self into the realms of the west, whose gateways we opened and whose energies were availed to us from our mighty allies in the realm of the element of water.

Immediately you sense the power of this element and are almost overwhelmed by the feeling. It seems denser than the others, but remarkably dynamic. Time is slower here and your perception of time slows. Nothing matters, there are no deadlines or worries, all cares are washed away or flow out of you as you relax completely. The hurried expansive energy of the first two quarters is a memory as now you feel the energy condensing. Again you are aware of entities moving and wafting around you in slow motion. The undines take many shapes and form, regarding you with many alien eyes. You fear not as you are in the realm of mighty allies and friends. This intelligence watches you and cares for you, allowing you to sense this realm but watching over you in the density of its slow motion and unpredictable forces.

Now you realise that you are looking out over the same landscape as before, however now you discern the element of water permeate deeply and carry the first two forces, helping to both ground these into a denser form and allow their energies to be transmuted across the landscape. There is an uplifting emotion permeating all, as this element infuses and dissolves at all corners, allowing life to function.

Again the Goddess speaks:

"I am the water and blood of life. In me is the purity of ages. My love descends to physical form and rains down into every pore. I am needed and give freely; I am lover to the parched earth who aches for me, nourishing the delicate flowers and pit-a-pat the scorched earth with hope ever after. I alone gush forth and bring all life, for all time. There are no other Gods where I am. Blessed are you my priestesses and priests who sip at the cup of the water of life."

You feel the cleaning water; the energy of Lammas flow through your body and aura. The healing and energy flow everywhere, seeping into all parts; giving life and removing negativity, leaving you refreshed and feeling clean, light and new; yet another gift from your allies in the realm of water. You see the waters swell into the grain, giving all the plants life. You realise how much of an ally the west has become to you as you thank them as old friends and depart back to the solidity of the circle. You feel like you want to remain there, in the floating slow motion and care-free realms, though you know you have more to see and do.

You now return to the sitting position within the circle. You take a few seconds to collect yourself before the journey continues.

Now that you have returned to the solidity of the circle, we now focus on the north. This time you send your astral self into the realms of the north, whose gateways we opened and whose energies were availed to us from our mighty allies in the realm of the element of earth.

As you walk into the north, you see the distant jagged mountain peaks beyond; the solid crunch of earth beneath your feet is sturdy and reassuring. You walk further in and you sense the power of this element. It has a mysterious quality that the others do not quite convey. You know there is magick and mystery here. This is a world of many shamanic allies and powerful Gods and Goddesses. Again the north seems more dense than the east or south, but remarkably dynamic. Time is more normal here and familiar to you. There is a real feeling of solidity and perfectly condensed energy as again you sense entities moving and walking around. They squirm and mould the earth around them. The gnomes of the world are hard at work and barely notice you. Many entities move and burrow and walk around you. You fear not as you are in the realm of mighty allies and friends. This intelligence watches you and cares for you, allowing you to perceive this realm but watching over you in the shadowy cool realm of the north.

Again you realise that you are looking out over the same landscape as before. However, now you sense and feel the landscape as a very real place and you know you are seeing somewhere close and relevant to you.

The power of the one thing, transmuted by the other three forces, finds expression here and again is transmuted further by life and death. This realm feels mysterious to you as here are some of the greatest mysteries you also face in your lifetime. As you think of this again the Goddess speaks:

"I am the red-ochre blood substance of the earth. Here is my body, my strength my anger and my beauty. Hunter and hunted in both hands. I am the strike and the trill scream in the night and I sing a dirge lamenting song in the morning. Terrible to behold for some am I; red gore and freedom and death. I caress the weak and hold everything in my embrace, both terrible and lovely to behold. All things are begotten in my womb and therein all things shall return. There are no other Gods where I am. Blessed are you my priestesses and priests who walk on the paths best set with my knowledge and power."

You feel the strength of Lammas flow through your body and aura. The healing and energy flow everywhere, solidifying in your aura as if the gnomes have made armour for you from the best materials. You feel stronger than you have ever felt before; another gift from your allies in the realm of earth. You see the nutrients of the life supporting soil give to the plants, that which it could not support on its own. You realise how much of an ally the earth elementals have become to you as you thank them as old friends and depart back to the solidity of the circle. You felt like you wanted to remain there, in the strong, solid mystical realm, though you know you have more to see and do.

You now return to the sitting position within the circle. You take a few seconds to collect yourself before the journey continues.

As you ponder what you have learned about the alchemy of the season and the transduction of the one thing linking them all, you realise that the fifth element, spirit was present in each quarter. The realisation of this thrills you as you begin to work out how each element relies on another and both spirit and energy moves between them. You watch as, in the circle you see before you, an image of Brigid's cross linking all the four quarters appears. It spins faster and faster as you hear her speak inside your mind:

"I am the power throughout the universe and the power within. I am as above as so below. I am your reality as I was before and beyond your very existence. I have been with you from the beginning and will find you at the end. I am the transformer of life and soul. There are no other Gods where I am. Your soul has walked a journey of realisation this Lammas with me. I was the catalyst binding them all and you who were split in twain in Litha have been made whole again! Rejoice; blessed are you who contemplate the love of me, the desire and will of nature. To grow, to have liberty, to have life."

Understanding this moment, you thank this mighty Goddess. Taking your right hand to your neck and shoulder you say:

"I thank you Goddess Brigid. I am no longer guilty!"

You sit and relax and feel the gifts of the elements coursing through you, linking you to the very planet itself, making you feel whole again. Eventually you hear the distant chiming in the circle and, taking your time, slowly return to the circle or place of comfort. The chimes will ring nine times and you will collect yourself calmly back into the room during this time. When you are ready, focus on the altar candle to ensure you are fully back to waking consciousness and that all parts of your mind are back to our time and space.

Goddess Brigid Internal Power Charge (see page 7).

Mabon

"When day-time and night-time are equal, When sun is at greatest and least, The four Lesser Sabbats are summoned, And Witches gather in feast."

DOREEN VALIENTE (*Witchcraft for Tomorrow*)

To Consider: It is a time of equal day and equal night when nature is in balance. It is a time to reap what you have sown, of giving thanks for the harvest and the bounty the Earth has provided. You should consider aligning your energies with that of the planet at this time to finish the projects you have been working on and plant the seeds for new enterprises or a change in lifestyle. Mabon is a time of reflection and balance.

It may be a temptation to overdo things or rush to finish, but also remember there is balance and so relaxation and enjoying the fruits of your labours must also be built into your plans.

Mabon Alchemy: At Mabon we make progress with **Operation 4: Conjunction – Union**. Quite simply the happy union we have willed and initiated at Lammas with the forces of spirit continue as we celebrate the time of thanks and balance.

Dennis William Hauck in the *Azoth Ritual* provides us with invaluable insights into this stage/operation:

> *"The alchemists often referred to the Conjunction as the 'Marriage of the Sun and Moon,' which symbolised the two opposing ways of knowing or experiencing the world. Solar consciousness is intellectual and relies on rational thought; lunar consciousness is feeling-based and taps into non-rational sources of information like psychic impressions and intuition.*
>
> *Physiologically, Conjunction is using the body's sexual energies for personal transformation. Conjunction takes place in the body at the level of the Heart Chakra. Psychologically, Conjunction is empowerment of our true selves, the union of both the masculine and feminine sides of our personalities into a new belief system or an intuitive state of consciousness."*

Mabon Ritual Template.

A lit altar candle for focus.

Goddess Brigid Internal Power Charge (see page 7).

Power: The Rune and/or transactional magick.

One, all or three people: Recite the words of the poem to honour and guide in the Goddess. Three chimes (for the triple Goddess) are given at the start to prepare the mind for the meditation. Each Stanza could be given to a different person for a collaborative effect. The final stanza is followed by three = nine.

Mabon Poem/Offering of words: Offer palms outwards towards the centre of the altar (e.g. statue, veve, symbol) which represents Brigid! Feel the power and imagery flowing towards her as praise and offerings.

All: Mighty Goddess we both honour you and evoke you with these words.

Mystery, of 'Mabon little seed' is 'the one thing' kept,
Ap Modron the Angel – mother, within her you slept.
Bite through the core to a secret of Kore there concealed,
Of a message the tablet of emerald revealed.
Not one forever perished; the one thing is reborn,
As sure as it rises each summer with corn.

Plentiful harvest again will she bestow,
Mother, she blesses us as above so below.
On bended knee, from our hearts this night we give thanks,
Demeter, Persephone, Dionysus, Hermes and all Gods in your ranks.
Restore us with the grain, grape and this bounty the harvest
provides,

On this night of balance, in this place where your power resides.
Now we rejoice in your Magick, so mote it be.

All: Great Goddess Brigid – lead us peacefully through this Mabon Pathworking.

Mabon Pathworking: As you relax in the circle you begin to reach out to the energies of the season again. There is a feeling of plenty and reward. Music and merriment are the order of the day. In the incense-filled room as you feel the energies of the day, you have a sense of the many other Mabon Sabbat celebrations which have occurred in Wiccan circles. They too met in such circles and danced, drank and spoke the words.

Another image comes to you now. In the circle you begin to make out the swirl of the astral light within the incense. You are about to ready yourself – to send yourself into the astral realm for the next guided meditation – but wait, perhaps there is no need.

For as you sit still in this room, you see in your mind's eye the image of a person begin to take shape in the astral mist that whips along the floor and around the circle like willow the wisps of smoke. The image is as thin as gossamer on faint moon beams, but clearly there is somebody there, or rather something.

Sounds clatter in the distance, which may be the hallway or outside the window – you are not sure. It is the sound of hoof on the ground, like a mighty stallion coming near. The sound is a little disconcerting, especially as it echoes here and there and does not seem to have a direct location.

You feel a little apprehensive of the figure now taking shape in the midst. It is tall and strong, erect and imposing. What look like long pointed antlers project out of each side of his head, held up by a strong muscular neck and huge powerful body. Something like a large skin is draped over his head and shoulders and hangs down to his feet. The smell of moss and greenery fills your nostrils. The raw power of nature assails your senses. Instinctively you look down, afraid to be seen by this giant, powerful mass.

You feel a little afraid by this spirit's presence as its power is quite palpable but feels unpredictable and capable of wanton destruction if given free reign. Unlike the Goddess, this power does not feel wholly human or that it should be concerned with any aspects of humanity at all.

The figure makes a sound that sounds like booming thunder – but in your mind you hear the words:

"I am happy with your efforts. I was the one who started the building of this temple in my lands many moons ago. You heard the call, wise ones – wiccans you are – but I call ye the people of the world tree!"

You realise that at this Sabbat, as with many others, you may have called on the Horned God to be a part of the rite; to have his presence talking though a High Priest. Though now you consider that we have not played out a rite to celebrate and connect with the Sabbat of Mabon! A slight anxiety passes through your mind, have we done enough for Mabon?

But the mighty spirit that remains before you in the circle, which now resembles some sacred spot or glade in an ancient forest, knows your thoughts.

"If you would not have laboured hard or laboured at all then there would be no Mabon night! Yet here we stand again! Here my Priests and Priestesses know my mysteries; the sap of the tree has risen, as was ever so. If I fall this night into the mother of us all, I fall only from your sight; I will loosen the veil once again."

The Horned God figure shows you an image of himself dying in ecstasy. But this image now, like a dream, becomes a feeling which electrifies your body like a static jolt which sharpens all your senses to a clear point of consciousness. You recognise a feeling that is always present within you. You recognise this as a life force and moreover a very human life force. With the God's consciousness racing through your own aura now you understand that nothing else, no artificial intelligence in some great computer, no God, no other entity in existence has this precise expression of this feeling of the life force – only you. The goat-God speaks:

"I wear many faces, all are shadows of the other, light and dark, life and death are mirrors by which we view each one."

He beckons you to follow him and your astral body rises and walks behind the huge dark figure striding into the darkness. You feel as if you are in some kind of Neolithic forest deep in the ancestral mind of our species. Further we walk, winding through foliage and blackness. Small flowers beam here and there – almost illuminous and ghost-like with their white radiant petals dotted across the landscape like stars in the night sky. Occasional dog-violet flowers in patches stake their claim; their droopy purple hued petal heads flopping over, catching the night breeze, periodically jolting lightly in the dark by the unseen hand of air. Wild roses, like the dog-rose climber, beam reddish hues in the foliage, like many red-tinted eyes watching you in the darkness. Many small flowers of enchanter's nightshade coolly stare up innocently from the carpeted forest's fern covered floor. Instinctively you understand something of its intoxicating power, as the presence of the God teaches you the ways of the wood as you walk. You respect and now somewhat revere these power plants – each one you see now as a daemon's physical presence in this world.

The sweet smell of honeysuckle clings to the air tinged with a fox – like mustiness from the many small flowers. Many of these plants seem to hum with electrical forces, like the life force coursing through them at this time.

As you walk, you begin to sense heat and the smell of wood smoke assails your nostrils. Eventually you come to a clearing where a huge fire burns in a large circular area. The horned figure moves like some old shamanic priest towards the fire and takes a seat. He then gestures towards some red flowers growing at the edge of the circle. You can see pinkish-red flowers with five almost heart shaped petals stretching up from the ground to about half a meter high.

The God form stretches down and cups a flower in the palm of his hand.

"This is the female flower of the little flower named for my name-sake Sileneus you will know it as Red Campion."

He then cups another:

"And here is the male flower!"

You are fascinated as you look closely at each flower, their delicate heart shaped petals seem unreal to you. As if these were made with the story of the Gods of the ancient woodland written in the foliage in plain sight for you to read and understand. You think to yourself, 'how come no-one has really noticed this before – this cannot be a coincidence surely...!'

The God, as if reading your mind, answers your thoughts;

"Five petals there are – three for our lady and two for my shadow selves; the Green Man and the Lord of Shadows. See their hearts call to each other across the green – and nature moves in concert; the sap has a will and the drunken dance of life is glorious once again."

Again you look closely, captivated by all the detail in this little flower. You feel enthralled that a physical emblem of your spiritual belief system actually exists, quietly sustained in the dark forests, hedgerows and even the gardens within the bustling cities a few feet away from all the unaware people walking by. Your eyes trace all the fine hairs over the downy stem, to the fine detail of each petal, each vein. Small dappled spots of white exist in the pinkish hue; a small crown in the centre contains the male anthers and pollen lies within. Even the crown is a small emblem of this mighty spirit of nature, you muse to yourself – how amazing!

You touch the flower in an effort to communicate with the spirit of the species itself. Immediately a voice enters your mind:

"I am like the crown of your consciousness… I am like your rational self."

You look over at the image of the mighty God who remains still by the fire; he seems to smile back knowingly and then gestures to the other flower. You look excitedly at the female flower and again feel in awe of the detail you can see. This is a larger flower, though despite this you can 'feel' its femininity. In the centre, five delicately curved styles and stigma protrude, like strange velvet art exhibits. Again you venture to gently touch one, to make contact with the group mind of the species again. Immediately there is a sentence searing through your mind;

"I am like the heart of your intuition… I am like your instinctual self."

You look over at the God again who is smiling and now he speaks into you mind;

"The little red power has much to teach you today."

You look again at the flowers and cup the female flower in your left hand while the right hand finds the male flower. You feel them grow around your wrist and tighten. You cannot move but you feel relaxed as the sound of the bonfire crackles in the night. You feel the essence of the plants in your mind again.

You see the Horned God lift a mighty blade from his side and you wonder for a moment whether he will cut some of the foliage with it to place into the cauldron which lies a few feet away from the fire. Instead, he raises the sword high into the air before turning it downwards towards the vessel saying the words you recognise.

"As the sword is to the Male, so the Cauldron is to the female; so, conjoined, they bring blessedness."

You smile at the recognition of this symbolic rite but before you can think further another voice sinks into your brain from the little red power plant;

"Conjoined they are anew, one!"

It is like the female aspects have met the male aspect of the power plant, spirit ally, and little red power campion within your very soul. Quickly you feel a rapid expansion of your consciousness, and feel the truth in the words. Your rational self has melded with your heart self. Your intellect is now more in line with your true self – this union played out in the forest and the rekindling of the life force each time, you see now, is a template for your soul. A union of many parts to a new whole is both a universal truth and a divine one. Suddenly, you think of the words you have heard many times and so with renewed understanding you arise exclaiming the words!

"As above so below, praise Hermes, praise Silenus my Lord and her the Lady Brigid!"

With that the lord of the Greenwood smiles and nods over at you – taking up a large drum he beats rhythmically.

Your mind soars with a sense of your true will. You feel taller, more real and more powerful. You feel alive and capable of exerting all your energy into any project and life challenge yet to do. You understand you are here and alive and have a part to play. Now you can devote yourself to your own will and perform it willingly and creatively. You feel you want to live your life as the Goddess would have you do – wielding her power through your actions, aligning your will with that of the Lady for the good of your family, community and world.

Finally you exclaim, out loud:

"Mother Brigid, I forgive everyone including myself!"

The drum beats on and you sit in the circle enjoying the new found aspect of yourself, knowing that your spirit and aura are energised fully for the work ahead.

You listen to the drumming in the circle and taking your time; slowly return to the same sound within the room. Drums allow you to collect yourself calmly back into the room during this time. And when you are ready, focus on the altar candle to ensure you are fully back to waking consciousness and that all parts of your mind are back to our time and space.

Goddess Brigid Internal Power Charge (see page 7).

Samhain

"The Law of Darkness and Light states: As you are dark, I am light & as you are light, I am dark. This law speaks to the duality of nature and all beings within it, including human beings. This law speaks to balance, more specifically, balance within yourself."

ANASSA ROSE (*10 Most Important Laws for Successful Magick*)

To consider: Death! And other endings. Samhain is therefore not only a time for reflecting on mortality, but also on the passing of relationships, jobs and other significant changes in life. Samhain is a time for taking stock of the past and coming to terms with it, in order to move on and look forward to the future. Leaving old and unhelpful patterns behind and looking forward to a new bright start. This is as good a time as any for divination, harnessing the energies and influences around you and up ahead. Will! What can we will towards our own spiritual development and a happy rebirth of circumstances?

Samhain Ritual Template:

Lit altar candle for focus.

Goddess Brigid Internal Power Charge (see page 7).

Power: The Rune and/or transactional magick.

One, all or five people: Recite the words of the poem to honour and guide in the Goddess. Three chimes (for the triple Goddess) are given at the start to prepare the mind for the meditation. Each stanza could be given to a different person for a collaborative effect. The final stanza is followed by one = nine.

Samhain Alchemy: Laboratory Putrefaction begins with degradation followed by Operation 5: Fermentation and putrefaction. You can see this analogy in the making of beer, the yeast (a single celled mould) feeds on the crushed and malted barley. New life and a brand new product are created by this miracle of nature, a transformation of energy and a reinvigoration of the mystery of life. The idea of sacrifice and new beginnings is exactly what we understand by the death card in tarot. We fear this card, but really it belies a miraculous aspect of life's tenacity and alchemical processes. Therefore this notion is ideal for an association with Samhain.

Dennis William Hauck in the *Azoth Ritual* provides us with invaluable insights into this stage/operation:

"Fermentation starts with the inspiration of spiritual power from Above that reanimates, energises, and enlightens the alchemist. Thus, personal Fermentation is living inspiration from something totally beyond us. In society, the Fermentation experience is the basis of religion and mystical awareness."

Samhain Poem/Offering of words: Offer palms outwards towards the centre of the altar (e.g. statue, veve, symbol) which represents Brigid! Feel the power and imagery flowing towards her as praise and offerings.

All: Mighty Goddess we both honour you and evoke you with these word:.

Joy swells in the blackness, growing fat as a ripe pumpkin.
Pitted against the dark wet earth 'neath the cool tar-black air.
A last celebration of summer, orange and round, sides as bright
as the sun.
Beaming from the clods of mud, lit up on one side by a glare of
their fire.
Phosphorus and magnesium rip the air, revealing a world of
shadows.
All life is now hereby reduced to stark bright expression in a
fleeting moment.

The light has dropped, the mother she's turned her heart away
from him.

And dark has arrived, like swift inky raven wings quickly
plunging the early evening into the spirit realm.
The candle's flicker is all that is seen, as they tarry a moment
here and there.
It is said they hear us still, vying to speak but fading into dreams.
Have pity, have heart, how must it be to see everything and do
nothing?
Nothing but wait; treading softer than rain on a land that
ignores their will.

Morning mists hang heavy on the hay bales, as the light cools to
a crisp white glow.
Soil fingers grasp, holding onto bare bones of dead vegetative
bodies.
Seeping and absorbing all with the final breath of sleep and sink
back into the mud.
Stillness slowly descends; like the deadness that follows
yesterday's parties.
Hay and stem, leaves litter like ticker tape on the pathways.
Instinctively we gratefully celebrate the old year that carried us
and yearn for the new life waiting beyond.

We do not fear the dark, for she, the Cailleach Beara awaits us
there. Watching us stumble, keeping the road for us.
The Queen of Night also knows the way ahead.
The old fears die and the new will is forged.
Death creates the world and like the two faced God Janus,

instinctively we feel in Samhain the moment of creation. And a time to remember and sorrow whilst also renewing the pledges and celebrating all.

Hail to the Goddess!
Hail Brigid!
Hail Cailleach!
Hail HeKate!

All: Great Goddess Brigid – lead us peacefully through this Samhain Pathworking.

Samhain Pathworking: As you sit quietly in the circle you stretch out your senses into the night and thence into the astral mists, closer to us now and easier to enter. This may be the Sabbat you feared, this may be the Sabbat which brings you feelings of sadness and loss!?

What mighty Goddess, what terrible Daemon will guide your hand in this lesson? Will Hekate form from the very material of darkness itself, as she has done so before, and cradle us with her enveloping dark wings? Will the crone, dreadful in her appearance, talk to us of the harshness of life and make us confront things we tend to ignore or facts we would rather avoid? Could he Horned One take us by the hand and show us the meaning of death and rebirth?

Slowly you are compelled to look towards the altar (either present or in mind) where you notice the picture of a kindly looking older woman. She is happy to be in the company of others and you sense she is or was a High Priestess of Wicca. She is High Priestess Cailleach from a coven from the north east of Scotland many moons past.

You regard the face of High Priestess Cailleach happy and content having come to terms with both the mystery of life and death. As you look upon the face of the woman, you notice that her eyes seem to move and focus upon you a little more. You rightly feel scared at such an event and you observe the picture further. It is now that you realise that High Priestess Cailleach is indeed staring at you but with both affection and knowing. You know in that moment that she supports followers on the path of Wicca still. Silently you walk towards the picture on the altar for a closer look and are astonished that High Priestess Cailleach hands you a card. You look to see the death card in your hands. You look back at High Priestess Cailleach awaiting more answers but the picture is now as it was.

You return to your seat and regard the card. As you do so the image of the card fills your consciousness and becomes a doorway to the symbols represented therein. You are transported at high speed to a small peaceful strip of land for which you feel some recognition. It is cold and barren as the wind relentlessly whips over the shortened stalks and earth laid bare beneath your feet. Looking around you, your memory is jolted to the Lammas Sabbat where you saw this place alive with crops and the dance of the elements. All lies still as cool moist air settles on the earth with the finality of an outbreath of a forest slowing down to a phase of imperceptible life. Curiously a hooded, robed figure walks towards you, striding with confidence and purpose; he/she begins to speak, strangely uninvited, without even an introduction.

"You can learn much from the forest, all the many trees and plants vie for the light. Some grow fast and tall and shade others in their wake. But look, the slower growing oak thrives over time while the fast Birchwood loses the grip of life to become the compost of the forest's mossy – carpet floor. The sap rises and the life forces spiral through to a wonderful expression of a cacophony of harmonious variety, of ecosystems in balance."

You understand what the wise figure has told you and, as he or she speaks, you can see the very serpentine earth-energy etched as spirals in the xylem of all vascular plants. You think to yourself – 'Yet how can all this harmony exist? Each and every organism is selfishly drawing nutrients and pushing as fast as they can in an explosion of greenery and bright flowering sparks of fertility, playing out in slow motion. The jostling and yielding species are eager and desperate for a share of the limited resources of nature.

You understand the genetic 'will' set in clockwork motion programmed by death and defeat – survival of the fittest. Yet she mourns for the dead, our Lady Brigid, she tends the sick and by showing us her role as healer, she gives us the knowledge that all life should be given a chance to express itself. The Gods and other elemental spirits, you see, are the tenders; the shepherds and the gardeners of the energy of life expressing its will from whence it came.

Thus chaos does not reign, harmony arises and ecosystems are in balance and the concerto of life blossoms in every corner of the world. Likewise, each person has the right to do their will and no other shall say nay! Each person has the right to healing and a guiding hand in their lives, should they will it! Though, you ponder, if that is true, why indeed is there evil and chaos in the world? Again the person speaks;

> *"We can learn much from the forest – see all the different plants raise their kundalini life forces and vie for the light. Yet there is paradise. Would it be so that if all human beings were to raise the serpent life force, and understand that they could do as they will, yet no others shall say nay, then each delicate flower and each mighty oak could live in peace, live in paradise. Dead leaves cast from the bough shall again nourish and make the self-anew."*

You realise that the allegory has gone from the forest to the people and to you. You feel something like a coat slip from your shoulders and hit the earthy ground with a soft crumpled thud. You see on the floor around you an old crumpled coat looking like a pile of leaves or foliage on the earth. As you look around for the priest or priestess who was speaking to you – you understand in a flash that the person talking under the hood is in fact yourself and that that very cloak has been abandoned and is now the same pile you regard on the earth.

The lesson you sense immediately is that you didn't need any extra guidance or lessons from the land of the dead, but now

after so many Sabbats and circles, you have become the priest/
priestess, wise-one, the shaman and you have the knowledge of
alchemy. You are the best teacher you will ever have! You walk
away from the cloak which you abandoned. This garment's fate
is to putrify and become anew, you know this and fear it not, you
are the illuminated Wiccan walking back into the physical world
of women and men.

As you walk, you stretch your awareness up as far as you can
and consider the aspect of allowing others the chance to find
their will or path in life. Perhaps your own actions have invariably
affected others either directly or indirectly, such is the way of the
modern world, so you raise your arms up and exclaim to our
mother Brigid;

"Please forgive me for any mistakes I have made!"

The sound of the chime gently rings eleven times and you sit
in the circle enjoying the knowledge that you have gained better
self-awareness. You feel this strengthen yourself, your aura and
make you become more 'in the world'.

You listen to the chimes in the circle and taking your time;
slowly return to the same sound within your place of comfort.
The soft chiming allows you to collect yourself calmly back into
the room during this time. And when you are ready focus on the
altar candle to ensure you are fully back to waking consciousness
and that all parts of your mind are back to our time and space.

Goddess Brigid Internal Power Charge (see page 7).

Yule

To Consider: Hope for the self – yourself. The rebirth of the Sun, the longest night of the year and the Winter Solstice brings introspection and planning for the future. Contemplate Brigid's light shining in the darkness, illuminating your soul with the joy of Christmas/Yule morning. The choirs are celebrating the return of the Sun. Family and friends celebrate, give gifts and share the festival of the return of energy, the return of life and the celebration of this life that runs through the family, friends and community. We must take back this festival from the profane, who claim it, represents one King only. This is a festival of all these Kings and Queens of the Sun and Earth.

Yule Alchemy: This is a time of reflection and spiritual celebrations which is associated with **Operation 6: Distillation**. Perhaps it is very fitting indeed to link distillation with this time of the year, as in the laboratory, distillation is the heating and re-condensing of the fermented solution to increase its purity and strength. In terms of the barley making beer at Samhain, we now go further and create the whisky at Yule.

Dennis William Hauck in the *Azoth Ritual* provides us with invaluable insights into this stage/operation:

"Distillation is the purification of the unborn Self -- all that we truly are and can be..."

"Physiologically, Distillation is raising the life force repeatedly from the lower regions in the cauldron of the body to the brain (what Oriental alchemists called the Circulation of the Light), where it eventually becomes a wondrous solidifying light full of power. Distillation is said to culminate in the Third Eye area of the forehead, at the level of the pituitary and pineal glands, in the Brow or Silver Chakra. On the Planetary level, Distillation is the realization of the power of higher love, as the life force on the entire planet gradually seeks to become one force in nature based on a shared vision of Truth."

Yule Ritual Template:
Lit altar candle for focus.
Goddess Brigid Internal Power Charge (see page 7).

Power: The Rune and/or transactional magick.

One, all or six people: Recite the words of the poem to honour and guide in the Goddess. Three chimes (for the triple Goddess) are given at the start to prepare the mind for the meditation. Each stanza could be given to a different person for a collaborative effect. This will make nine.

Yule Poem/Offering of words: Offer palms outwards towards the centre of the altar (e.g. statue, veve, symbol) which represents Brigid! Feel the power and imagery flowing towards her as praise and offerings.

All: Mighty Goddess we both honour you and evoke you with these words:

Lamplight beckons in the yuletide; a once sun kissed world now
rattles and shrieks against the window.
She scorns the night, dancing in the crisp snow.
Clattering upon the dark paths, the whipping howling winds are
his feet.
His crown of holly shakes in defiance at the storms as he faces
death.
His power forged anew with the elements; this spirit of nature.

We reclaim this night for them!
Lord and Lady, King and Queen.
And on the darkest day, what joy they make in that miracle
morning.
Time stands still while magick fills the whole sky,
we breathe it into our heart through zinging cold nostrils.

We feel this celebration of love, family and life.

Instinctively they praise their God on this day;

And Mithras before that, because;

As the yuletide moves through the world, through every beast, child, woman and man,

The mystery of mysteries weaves through the two, to the three and for a moment one.

Her lithe ivy wraps in spirals across the sinew-woody body of his form.

The glorious holly, swelled red pearls are drops of dew from the lover's secret sweet scent.

Glinting like a rash across the icy world. Life over death, love over chaos.

And so on this morning, the wise see that if love can always triumph this morning and evermore.

The dark cannot extinguish the light and his spirit burns bright forever.

They whisper to you; "It has been revealed that love is the law, love under will. Know our spirits are within you also…"

The choirs should ring with joy all this day!

Forever in ecstasy to you, to you forever, forever always Brigid.

All: Great Goddess Brigid – lead us peacefully through this Yule Pathworking.

Yule Pathworking: At Samhain you realised that you had become your own master. You now find yourself walking along a familiar street from your youth. It is the holiday season. You are filled with anticipation of what this Yule will bring. The wonder you feel has instilled in you a feeling of magick and possibilities that you have never felt at any other time of the year, until now. You accept this feeling that anything is possible and magick fills the very air we breathe. Everybody shares this feeling of excitement, though if asked, who can pin-point the source? Who can definitely explain the exact nature of it? Only that it is understood that this sensation stretches back into antiquity back to European mediaeval times and then further back perhaps to Mithraic spiritual practices of the Romans around the 1st century B.C.. And then of course further back hundreds of years before that, to old Persian notions of spirituality and further back, spiralling into the mists of time.

You have found yourself standing still on that street from your nostalgic past and, like a dream, time stands still. The cold crisp air stings your face and a white hue fills the air. You begin to make out two shapes in the mist. Both are human in form though much bigger and taller. You do not feel scared or have any compulsion to run; instead you watch the scene with some fascination and wonder; the same sense of wonder that is felt at this time of year is with you still. The figures loom, a clearer perspective now. The figure on the right is tall and strong dressed in pure white robes. His antlered head stands tall in the white mist. The female figure on the left is also dressed in white with a smaller antlered head or head-dress; creating a silhouette against the white mists swirling behind them. There is a real chemistry, a strong and palpable sexual tension and obvious close bond exists between them. You realise that the female Goddess figure appears to hold her belly in such a way as to suggest that she is pregnant. However you notice that she is not holding her belly as such, though instead is cradling a large and very bright ball of white light. She nurtures the light between her hands, and it does not appear to harm her in any way.

The God figure seems to understand your mind and you muse that this was also the case before, when you met a version of him in the wood at Litha. He speaks:

> *"The anticipation you feel is the anticipation of the life of the world. It is the anticipation of the coming of the Sun. Many names have been given; many dresses have been clothed on the day of the ultimate expression of this magick!"*

You suddenly understand in that instant what nature has been showing you from the start. As you look upon the loving grin appearing on the powerful visage of the kingly figure looming before you, you know in your heart that there are strong forces of love pulsing over our planet in these yearly cycles. This interplay has been operating since long before Mithras and long before ancient homo-sapiens or even before any species of homo species stood upright at all. Before even, the reptiles dominated and clung to life and long before the carboniferous age of forests absorbed the early Sun's energy and even before the inchoate forms of life absorbed the earliest gasses and kissed the early winds with oxygen-death before sustaining life again. The powerful voice in the mists joins your thoughts:

"Aye even before that..!"

Again you comprehend completely. The great God-force we call 'Time' has articulated this love and instituted the evolution of the God and Goddess through the countless eons. Humans are made in the image of the Gods...as we are natural expressions of them!

The images of the two dissolve from view but you feel them still and you are more aware that the feeling of Yule, the anticipation, is a real articulation of a certain energy which bubbles forth across the very solar system, in whose womb we are also carried; itself part of an even stranger mystery yet to be perceived by us all.

The feeling of both the God and Goddess are with you and their energies rise and reverberate within you still. Suddenly you feel the two polar energies smash and intertwine and you gasp as a liquid sensation collides and coils, pleasingly travelling upwards towards the heaven in your brain. Your mind and soul are capitulated strongly upwards and, like a scene of some shamanistic ecstasy, your soul self is lifted upward out of the top of your body out of the top of your head.

You are filled with an intensity of pleasure and power as your mind opens enough to encapsulate the rising kundalini, but not too much as to alter you too much, without you being able to cope with it – Lady Brigid the Goddess of change and illumination is both with you and watching you along this process – as she always has.

Your mind has ascended to higher realms such as the vapour of the body of the God during the distillation of the barley in the process of making whisky. You see that it is perhaps no coincidence that this process is perfected within this dark and holy realm we call Scotland. You think of the concept of 'the angels share,' and just as you are thinking this, you comprehend that you are in the company of angels. At that moment you understand that you have perhaps a temporary but direct link to your own Holy Guardian Angel.

You take a moment to reflect on this – what do you see/hear?

The company of angels, however beautiful, is at an end and now you find yourself in your own space – in your own body. However much you wish to be transformed by the circle of Sabbats is up to you. For you may realise, completely, that you have the right to do as you will.

So you raise your eyes up and exclaim to our mother Brigid;

"Mother, Lady and Lord – thank you for giving me my self-realisation!"

You feel very happy and lucky to be touched by the divine in this way. You sense a real celebration ringing around your world. The sound of the distant bells tolling is in rapture and the rebirth of the Sun and life as we know it. You muse to yourself, with your new-found illuminated sense of realisation on the interplay between the polarity of male and female, that the round curving waist of the bell and the curving receptive inner bow are like the female, while the active 'male-like' energy transduction action of the clapper, together celebrate these two opposites with the peel of sound echoing into reality.

Life, you understand, is a constant gift that we are given for absolutely nothing. Something for nothing (that never happens in our society), is continually created and re-created for our benefit. Knowing this, you feel delighted at the knowledge of our Earth, our mother selflessly giving and therefore, we in turn should honour that gift. However, you already know this, you have embarked already to heal and teach others.

Acknowledging this, look towards the area where you sensed the Gods. Meditate and feel the breeze of life arise and travel through your body, bringing further realisation and deeper understanding of yourself, nature and the Gods.

Eventually you listen to the pleasant sound of the yule-tide bells ringing and, taking your time; slowly return to the same sound within your place of comfort and protection. The soft chiming allows you to collect yourself calmly back into the room during this time. When you are ready, focus on the altar candle to ensure you are fully back to waking consciousness and that all parts of your mind are back to our time and space.

You are at one with the spirals of time and sense the coming of Imbolc with renewed optimism and confidence. So mote it be: Love is the law, love under will.

Goddess Brigid Internal Power Charge (see page 7).

Section Two

The Origins of Our Magick

"The birth and rebirth of all nature, / The passing of winter and spring, / We share with the life universal, / Rejoice in the magickal ring."

DOREEN VALIENTE

Wicca, of course, is the pagan religion which originated in Britain in the 1950s and is one of the fastest growing religions in the western world today. As observed by Professor Ronald Hutton, in his (splendid book) *The Triumph of The Moon*: "Modern pagan witchcraft is the only religion which Britain has given to the world."

Dr Gerald Brosseau Gardner (1884–1964) was an anthropologist, occultist and freemason. As a colonial in the Far Eastern service, he travelled widely, allowing him to pursue his deep intellectual and spiritual interests in folk magick of various cultures. He lived in Malaya and the Philippines and studied and participated in the folk magick practiced there. As well as this, he had an interest and exposure to relatively modern forms of Druidry, The Western Mystery Tradition as secretly transmitted through; the Rites of Masonry, the Rosicrucian orders, The Hermetic Order of the Golden Dawn and Ordo Templi Orientis (O.T.O). We know that Gardner had been given a charter to initiate members by the head of the O.T.O. Aleister Crowley in 1946 and that Gardner himself was (albeit technically only) European head of this Thelemic order in 1947.

Most modern evidence points strongly to modern Pagan Wicca emerging from the Bricket Wood Coven, near St Albans in Hertfordshire England in the early 1950s. Gerald Gardner and Edith Rose Woodford-Grimes (affectionately known as 'Dafo' by Gardner) likely instigated the initial format of the Wiccan religion. This masonic-style initiatory degree system was probably strongly influenced by the grading system of the O.T.O. Later, Doreen Valiente contributed much that informs the familiar practices we know today.

In my view, Wiccans attempt to recognise polarity in nature not as simply good versus evil, but as a more integrated and dynamic flow of energies. These aspects of reality, I believe, can be observed both within nature herself and within our own psyche. This places our brand of spirituality away from a simple light versus dark (good versus evil, and so on) but towards integration, in line with the aims and discoveries of modern humanistic psychology (the goal of self-actualisation, continual growth and lifelong learning). Many like myself are attracted to this perspective as Wicca obviously also encourages personal liberty! My perspective is therefore very much in line with Wiccan scholar and writer Vivianne Crowley, for example, who interprets the initiation degrees and rites of Wicca in terms of Jungian psychology, or the well-known practitioners and writers Janet and Stewart who see Wicca as an initiation process of growth and renewal.

As a matter of fact, I would state that the notion of good versus evil is where some new–age followers may tend to get a little too hung up on. To my mind, I believe that some of the new-age preoccupations with karma and light is just an extension of the old organised religious framework of the duality of good versus evil. Many Wiccans and others on the fringe of the new-age movements baulk at the idea of working with the Goetia or Demonolatry and similar practices! This is an attitude which could be comparable to the infernal notions of Voodoo experienced by early Christian missionaries in Africa; a reaction fundamentally borne out of misunderstanding and negative stereotyping. Ironically, such an attitude may rob many Wiccans of access to their own heritage. The old Gods and Goddesses we cherish today were similarly demoted to be the infernal Spirits and Demons by the invading dominator religion. Many of those new-age individuals I have generalised about would happily perform ceremonies devoted to a goddess, such as Aradia or Diana, whilst shunning those that investigate and utilise Demonolatry practices. Similarly many main stream religious people would accuse those participating in such ceremonies of being either no better or worse. And they would be right! There are many parallels with Demonolatry and Wicca (e.g. Aradia is the daughter of Lucifer and can be conflated with Hekate, the Queen of Night and Magick, perfect for working with demons and aspects of the dark and light). I definitely assert that all pagan paths could justifiably inform, utilise and share resources and magickal technologies with each other very effectively.

Wicca, as a spiritual path, tends to blur very easily with other new-age perspectives, but my opinion is that Wicca has at its heart a philosophy where nature is regarded in all its wonder, and beauty as well, as being red in tooth in claw. Nature may often be dark or fierce but that does not make nature and its God forms 'infernal'; rather the dark has to be acknowledged and understood, so that we may conquer, understand and consolidate our own vulnerabilities. I would also assert that Wicca is very much about embracing this reality, rather than shying away from it in a reclusive manner. Wiccans share a comprehension that real life, like the tarot deck, is complex and rather more 'grey' than mere black or white. Further, in my view, understanding the dark and grey within us and embracing this, rather than pretending it is not there, would represent real self-knowledge and growth as opposed to some fake and fluffy notion of forced goodness. The latter being an image or stereotype of certain new-agey types, who many Wiccans would prefer to distance themselves from.

We developed the following system of Sabbat workings by first using the original material I had acquired over the years from the Oldmeldrum Coven as a template with many additions of my own over the years that followed. In terms of the practice offered in this book, I also conclude that focusing on one or a very few spirits and one aspect of the Goddess (i.e. as Brigid) does help to streamline the process of working with the Alchemy of the seasons. As Wicca is a very eclectic spiritual path, with muddied origins, I also feel that clarifying a relationship with one mighty Scots/ British/European force of nature is much more beneficial in terms of strengthening an ongoing spiritual relationship (remember the ethos of transactional magick earlier in section one), as it is easier to focus your energies and thoughts on one person/spirit – rather than finding the time to honour many.

This is one of the things I think Wicca is 'for!' Wicca can serve the human alchemy of self-transformation as exemplified by the cycle of the seasons. This is invariably linked to our Wiccan notion of God and Goddess, of the natural alchemical idea of masculine and feminine polarities, in an ever dynamic dance of creation. Between them and with them flows the Earth-energy, the serpentine lines of kundalini awakening, flowing towards harmony and enlightenment. The same energies dwell within us just as we sense them awaken at Imbolc and flower and then transform to seed by Mabon, only to reside in the dark depths of the underworld during Samhain and Yule, ready to be reincarnated once again.

Obviously then, these Sabbats link backwards through time to antiquity and beyond! That is the idea we are drawn to at least, that this inherent 'truth' can be rediscovered and dusted free of years of church anti-propaganda, to be revealed in all its original beauty. A cherished ancient secret of humanness and libertarian freedom, diametrically opposed to the restrictive orthodoxy of the Church!

Well let's be open and honest and look at this, shall we? Wasn't it Robert Anton Wilson who said that intelligence that looks at itself is intelligence squared? On that note, RAW also said, and I quote: "Everyone has a belief system, B.S., the trick is to learn not to take anyone's B.S. too seriously, especially your own."

Sadly the Sabbats are not quite surviving relics of Gardner's Witch cult. In fact they come to us as assumptions based on the best speculation which circulated before more modern scrutinising archaeological academic historical research. The folklorist, anthropologist and Egyptologist, Margaret Murray (whom Gardner based much of his information on), gave us the notion of the Horned God and Goddess as well as the idea of an ancient system of fire festivals from 1917 onwards. This has now largely been debunked. A read of Doreen Valiente's *"Witch"*, the official biography by respected author Philip Hesleton, will also prove interesting, such as this passage;

"The specific details of the Craft rituals he had received from the New Forest coven were rather fragmentary in his memory and so he had been assembling written rituals from this and other material he found and researched. He was nonplussed when Doreen spotted the works of Aliester Crowley and Rudyard Kipling among Gerald's "Book of Shadows" and, in a fit of frustration, he apparently threw the book to her saying: "Can YOU do any better?" She reconstructed the writings, embellished

*and added to them with poetry of her own, and excised much
of what she described as "Crowleyanity" and when she had
finished, it seems Gerald realised they now had what he had
always wanted – a practical, logical, workable system of magick
and religion rooted in the traditions of British spirituality."*

So, no! Our religion has not survived the persecution of ages!
In fact Ronald Hutton has pointed out that, despite extensive
research; there is no actual proven link with some of the equinoxes
and ancestral pagan practices (e.g. Easter/Ostara). Though I will
emphatically observe that many of the Celtic traditions have been
preserved within Christian lore and practice, and we really must
kindly thank and appreciate the efforts of many Christian people
for this! (e.g. the Brigidine Sisters of Kildare in Ireland, who
tend a continual flame for St Brigid, a Christianised version of
our Goddess complete with her triple aspects as well). To quote
from writer Charlotte Allen in her 2001 article *The Scholars and the
Goddess*, "Practicing Wicca is a way to have Christianity without,
well, the burdens of Christianity." I would recommend a reading
of this article which appeared in the January 2001 edition of 'The
Atlantic'). I think it's time for many of us Wiccans to change our
mind-sets regarding our Christian brothers and sisters. Yes, there
are prejudices existing which harm our practice (I am frustrated
that in my professional life, I cannot be open about my preferred
spirituality or talk freely about my exercises in magick with my
colleagues and even some drinking buddies in the town where
I live). Though, I have found personal sources of prejudice to

come from the general public and even the media – not from the large majority of practising Christians.

However, it is interesting to me that the Wicca we know today therefore did develop in the 1950s and continues still as a response to the working environment! The members of the original Gardnerian coven were evidently and clearly not armchair magicians! Think… I bet you know quite a few?.

No, rather the early Bricket Wood coven were working ceremonial magick, Druidic inspired shamanic outdoor rites and basically calling the spirits to work with them, using whatever fragments of working 'Paganism' they could lay their hands on, and rekindled the sacred flame. Personally though, I am both satisfied and convinced that that is all it took to get it off the ground; their physical will, power and desire linking with the natural spiritual landscape. That's how magick works! You do it, you falter and learn and then you do it some more. I do not think that the original Bricket Wood coven would have lasted a year had they not put their hearts and souls into the magick. When you work with such powerful spiritual entities, an equally powerful feedback and spiritually alchemical process is put into play. I am assuming that those early practitioners would have had a lot of change, upheaval and ordeals to deal with in their lives as a result of engaging with such magickal forces, I am sure of that! Consider that Gardner's coven were linking and interacting with Goddesses and Gods. Not spirits of the dead, not servitors, nor even Angelic forms. Rather, the Goddess in all her forms and her consort God. As a magician who has worked with many classifications of spirit

I can tell you that there is not much more powerful a force in this universe, that I know of, than the Goddess (I call this one of the main powers or secrets of Wicca). Interestingly, my old High Priest (a man who was initiated by Gerald Gardner) stated the same thing to me about the ultimate power of the Goddess, many, many years ago, when I spoke with him about some banishing magick I had to perform. This does raise the question as to them (Bricket Wood) knowing exactly what they were dealing with at the time. If I were to summarise then, despite modern Wicca having its origins in wishful thinking and overly romanticised notions of pagan antiquity, the magick involved works! They (Bricket Wood) successfully re-booted the spiritual shamanic pagan current of the UK and northern Europe! This is because magick works! With enough intent and some grounding in the correct grimoires and practices, the natural intelligences involved respond! All practicing magicians in all traditions know this.

As there may not be a lineage to anything resembling a true witch cult, there are, however, well researched and understood lineages to definite magickal practices. Many magickal grimoires, such as *The Greater Key of Solomon*, *The Grimoire Of Pope Honorius*, The Greek papyri, Grecko-Egyptian magick, *The Goetia*, Qabalah, Tarot, Alchemy, Astrology and many other rites and practices fall into this genre. The witch cult we call Wicca was definitely re-booted in my mind very successfully from these and other inspirations. I include the Goddess (such as Brigid) as perhaps one of the major influences. If you doubt that Gardener, Dafo and co were successful, then look around!

So it is of no surprise to me that a formula of eight Sabbats crystallised from the Bricket Wood coven's on-going attempts to link with nature and indeed it does seem that that is exactly what happened, as the Sabbats we know today were effectively organised in early 1958!

> *"This situation ended in early 1958, when Gardner's main coven, based on the northern edge of London…Its members felt that the solstices in particular had great importance as calendar events, and that the equinoxes made a perfect symbolic balance for them. They therefore asked for equal observation of both the cardinal points of the Sun and the quarter days, as close to the actual dates as was conveniently possible. Gardner gave way, and in this manner the modern Pagan calendar of eight festivals came into being."*

Even if the religious aspects are dubious, we are still ceremonial magicians linked to the Western Mystery System thanks, in no small part, to Dr Gerald Gardner's thirst and search for knowledge. Here is what I think being a magician is:

1) To practice methods striving for illumination.
2) To work with spirit and the Divine.
3) To change themselves and ultimately reality.

A helpful note on practice and dealing with the spiritual realities in question: when the Greek and Egyptian magicians worked with nature and the magical beings on hand to provide them with spiritual and personal aid, they did not at any time consider these praeternormal intelligences as mere psychological constructs. When you work with a deity or spirit for any length of time, you too will begin to realise the limitation of thinking in the perspective of archetypes and mere psychological appendages that many modern practitioners have of spirits, angels and daemons. I would bid you to consider the wise words of Mr Charles Fort:

> *"I conceive of nothing, in religion, science, or philosophy that is more than the proper thing to wear, for a while."*

Around a hundred years ago, as a result of technology, mathematics and the observation of natural phenomena (such as steam engines either working or not working), we had the laws of thermodynamics which described the behaviour of the observable universe. Now we have quantum theory. In other words, our perceptions are 'squeezed' through the filter by the dominant perspective without us realising this. From my own experience, I think that you may well come at Wicca or Magick with such a typically very scientific perspective (as I did), though this will likely change in time. I propose that if we are to successfully use what we consider, rightly or wrongly, as our spiritual heritage, then we must build on and use the technologies in the grimoires (as mentioned above) as they were intended. That is, using magick respectfully, as if the spirits we evoke/invoke are separate conscious entities.

Fortunately, we can take some lessons from cultures which have not been corrupted by years of neglect or fragmentation of their native spiritual practices. I'm talking, in this case, about so-called ATRs (African Traditional Religions) which Gardner was also attracted to. Or the shamanic mind-set of the spirit aspect of nature. Take the following quote from *The Reality of Spirits*, By Edith Turner:

> *"Then I knew the Africans were right. There is spirit stuff. There is spirit affliction; it is not a matter of metaphor and symbol, or even psychology. And I began to see how anthropologists have perpetuated an endless series of put-downs about the many spirit events in which they participated—"participated" in a kindly pretence. They might have obtained valuable material, but they have been operating with the wrong paradigm, that of the positivists' denial."*

In this case Edith had been presented by seeing something in her reality which her Western perspective was ill-equipped to categorise or explain. Ordinarily, the average Western person would dismiss such an event. I believe engaging with our religion of Wicca can help us re-learn this aspect of nature, of walking once again with 'spirit.' You should know that there are apparently many in the ATR camp who view European magick e.g. Wicca with a little derision. Some think that our Western magick does not work as well because of gaps in our knowledge of how to approach spirits, how to live with them. Even Wiccans who make first forays into ceremonial magick such as Goetia do not always report great success. I think as Wiccans we could well be living and interacting with powerful daemons, Gods and Angelic forces on a day to day basis. As sorcerers, which is what we Wiccans are; we can be aware of nature spiritually all the time using pacts and allies. We probably are aware of synchronicities and spiritual life every day, not just at Sabbats or key circles. This, in my humble view is the go to the church on Sunday & switch off every other day model. I do not mean any disrespect to Christians, I know many feel their spirituality and derive very great strength from it on a continual daily basis. I think that the Wiccan desire to both interact and 'feel' the natural world spiritually can make us likely to sustain good relationships with the elementals who share the world with us. We personally, in the Circle of Brigid, place emphasis on mediumship and medium training, as much as ritual magick.

When we eat at each Sabbat within the circle, we are sharing the energy of the rite and the food with these 'presences' around us, which we have invited in. This is an offering. The flowers and the candles and the intention of the rite are also offerings. For example some beings like flowers, as they are beautiful and have scent, like incense and will absorb this. However flowers, especially cut ones are impermanent and some spirits will value this aspect also.

Candle light is also an offering in itself as most spiritual entities appreciate light. So the Sabbats are powerful points of interactions with our spirits, (again refer back to transactional magick in section one). Take this advice from *The Grimoire Abramelin the Mage*:

"Book II, Chapter 13

"Commence your prayer with fervour, for then it is that you will begin to enflame yourself in praying, and you will see appear an extraordinary and supernatural splendour which will fill the whole partment, and will surround you with an inexpressible odour, and this alone will console you and comfort your heart so that you shall call for ever happy the Day of the Lord."

Think of what we are doing with our brains!? What this technology is allowing us to do and see. You cannot inflame yourself in prayer if you are treating the phenomena as a psychological construct or a type of hallucination. To operate this type of magick correctly, then you must fully engage with it – immerse yourself in it and accept the technology for what it is. I'm sure this is why some people who participate in magick, such as Goetia, often fail. It is because they go into it with some preconception of disbelief and end up either working with a shade or psychological construct of the real thing, or place unconscious psychological barriers, preventing a link with the real thing. Think about it, if you go in concentrating, conjuring a mental construct – then that is what you will create/make/get. However, lose the mechanistic perspective (which is only a perspective), let the ego step aside and fully engage like the grimoire is trying to tell you to actually do, and wham! You'll go from shade-man to shaman in seconds. As long as you are sensible, and have the correct practice and protection, you will be fine.

This advice to 'enflame yourself with prayer' has been repeated often by the great Aliester Crowley! So here have we again a secret with regard to the efficacy of Wicca. The inherent religious aspect of the Wiccan magickal system allows us to ramp up our magick by having (often deep) personal relationships to mighty spirits. The closer and more nurtured the relationship may be, then the better it is. So, working closely and inflaming yourself with one Goddess, i.e. Brigid, as characterised by the rites in this book, will allow you, as a Wiccan practitioner, to connect with the Divine and therefore charge you magick. The fact that you are reading this and are willing to engage with the content is probably a step in that direction.

An Alchemical Formula

Usually a typical Wiccan rite will involve a script with words for participants to recite, as a kind of religious play, re-enacting a mythical aspect of the season. These are usually quite fun and help align members of a circle to connect with a particular 'pulse' of the season. Certainly we performed such rites at Oldmeldrum coven over the years, celebrating each turn of the wheel, as well as the later initial Circle of Brigid workings.

However, we of the next generation (Circle of Brigid) have experimented with altering this formula just a little. Incidentally, that is exactly what Marget Inglis of The Oldmeldrum Coven would have us do! She told me often to try to innovate and celebrate, rather than merely recite and reiterate!

I believe I now understand why Marget was keen to do this, as we have also noted during ritual re-enactment, having participants reading from a script only serves to distract people and, in some cases, unnerve people. I am sure if you are a high priest or priestess reading this, then you will understand exactly the types of scenarios that I am talking about! I have spent hours thinking and then writing what I consider to be the perfect words or symbolism of a particular verse only to end up smiling wryly to myself as participants strain to read the lines under dim light or argue amongst themselves about 'which bit they are meant to do' or which page they are on. Any import or impact that I originally intended, was now lost in the moment of hilarity of the emerging chaos. Now, hilarity is always fine! I remember Marget used to look at our young twenty-something contingent of the circle with affection and shrug, saying something like "laughter in a circle is never wasted energy and is a magick in its own right." Though I wonder now as the instigator of our own circle, was she thinking as I do; "...Although it is not exactly what I intended is it!?" So the rites I have presented contain a much reduced or minimal speaking contingent.

We have often graduated to a more stripped back formula which is thus:

1) Building energy (The Rune).
2) Transactional Magick.
3) Poem/Offering of words (for participation of members to add vocally as an offering of spirit and praises e.g. to the Goddess and the Gods of the season).
4) Any physical act – such as planting of seeds, healings, sigil work or working with the elements.

5) Pathworking – to connect with the seasonal tide at that Sabbat.

6) Cakes and ale (important to eat after the meditation to ground participants, socialise and relax back into mundane reality before jumping into cars or journeying home).

Brigid The Muse of Magick and Poetry

"she is my kind
and I like the warrior in her.
and I like when she carries her flag,
shouting what we still need to hear."

KARLA BARDANZA

As the Goddess Brigid is very well recognised as the muse of poetry in the Celtic mythology of these Isles, I was inspired to try to connect with her using poetic verses as my method in the rituals. I felt this would be more effective. I have only ever written a few lines of poetry now and again, though usually I am not overly inspired to write in this way. In other words, I do not consider myself a skilled poet, or profess to be, in any way. Though I feel like the mighty Goddess appreciates my efforts! Therefore, at each Sabbat, I have attempted to create a poetic aspect for inclusion in the ritual, which refers to aspects of that time of year. I believe this also provides a method of meditational practice to allow us to get into the right 'headspace' for the intended ritual working at that Sabbat. We have utilised this method throughout the wheel of the year on several occasions now, and they do serve as a useful start to proceedings. We at the Circle of Brigid can now attest to the fact that using these poems in this manner does indeed create a powerful and meaningful connection to Brigid. That is, they work! She appreciated the effort, and the effort makes her evocation much more likely and to be felt as a powerful presence in the room. I am also motivated to present these for use as, when I was writing earlier rites, I was frustrated that I could not always locate appropriate poems for the Sabbat. Therefore, writing my own tailor made verses was the perfect solution! So I would like to present these here for anyone to use as they see fit. However, by all means use these as a useful 'placeholder', but why not get to work creating your own (or as a group exercise), which can then serve the same function.

In the first instance, the poems are the opening focus of the rite, as they have been constructed to attempt to celebrate or characterise the aspect of the season or seasonal shift which the Sabbat represents. Used ritually, the words themselves are offerings which are given out to spirits. You can think of this as a form of praise aimed towards the Gods and Goddesses of the season, and/or the spiritual agents which we are interacting with at this time.

The method we find very effective is to first form a clear image in your mind of the spirit or astral realm which your mind has access to. Then actively project feelings of love and appreciation towards the Goddess and God. This has to be done with the intent of mutual co-operation with spirit. We believe it is better to have quite a shamanic mind-set here, where we want to both 'give' something back to these natural benevolent forces that are around us as allies, as well as to engender an ongoing relationship of trust and reward.

During the ritual, with the specific line you have to say aloud, consider how the words reverberate in the air. Remember, words carry 'intent.' Words are our primary magickal tool in any ritual or operation.

Of course, qabalistically-speaking there is a very direct relationship between the spoken word, sound and creation. The four letters of the Tetragrammaton (YHVH), the Hebrew word for God or Hashem, has an original meaning of "that which brings being into being." In fact this is also true for Hindu and Buddhist mystics, who believe that a word creates and pervades all existence. Therefore, giving both the heartfelt sentiment of the words of praise into the astral, along with the physical reverberation on the physical, is a great combination. Words are stamps of power, stamps of intent from the human mind onto the environment as physical waves of sound.

Pathworking –
The Paths Through
the Sabbats

"If you have time to breathe you have time to meditate."

AJAHN AMARO

Pathworking has been described by Michael York in *The A-Z of New Age Movements* as 'a form of collective meditation and a form of private hypnosis.' Also 'as a derivative of shamanism,' it very well may be. Certainly, any books I have read on shamanism seem to have, at the core of their journeying, an active imagination element, reminiscent of Pathworking. The name, of course though, refers to the paths linking the sephiroth on the qabalistic tree of life. As far as I am aware, such practices first came to light from authors such as Israel Regardie (e.g. *A Garden of Pomegranates*), as being the technique employed by Adepts of the Stella Matutina, to astrally explore the paths on the tree of life. This group was one of several off-shoots of The Hermetic Order of the Golden Dawn, after it fragmented in the early 1900's.

Pathworking, in its proper use, is a guided meditation that incorporates occult symbolism, mythological deities and attributes linking magickal concepts such as the tarot to the Hebrew alphabet and qabalistic sephiroth. Basically, the best way to think of the qabalah and the tarot is as similar to the notion of Yin and Yang but with a multi-layered patchwork of the many ordeals and life events in-between.

Pathworking is the shamanic perfect tool for the Wiccan Sorcerer. Journeying through the paths containing many relevant symbols of Wicca and the Sabbats, should allow us access to deeper aspects of our spiritual mind via the tool of imagination:

"Through the imagination… we can tap and release the energies of the Deep Mind to change ourselves .. to bring about changes in the 'external' reality around us"

PHIL HIND (Techniques of Modern Shamanism Vol II)

Pathworking was a practice utilised in the Oldmeldrum Coven from time to time, and it seems to have crept in more and more to the rituals as they have progressed with the Circle of Brigid. We have found that focusing the mind, using intuition and imagination in this way, really helps to create and kindle a personal experience in keeping with the particular focus of the rite. As I've stated, sticking to a script, in my view, only leads to some disconnection with the energies and the intent. Marget Inglis emphasised to us time and time again that the 'intent' was the most important aspect and not so much the 'actual exact words.'

I know of covens that make spectacular costumes and perform amazing theatre in places of power. In comparison, this approach must seem quite boring and seem in no way to be a better alternative. However, I would also argue that during such dramatic rites there would also be room for the poetic aspects presented here and the meditation aspect could be an interesting addition. The Pathworkings of Section One could even be acted out or performed in some way. Although, admittedly, my own opinion in this matter is that imagination is superior to acting or repetition of a script. Concentration of the mind, free from the distraction of 'lines,' can create a very personal astral aspect to the magick. If you are not as ingenious at 'cos play' or, like ourselves in the Circle of Brigid, have little time in your working week etc., to do this as often, or at all – then you may favour the meditational approach, as we do.

You would, however, benefit greatly from some key magickal hints and approaches essential to maximise a more beneficial experience, whilst engaging with the magickal practices outlined in this book and, indeed, any other magickal practice you undertake. There are many great authors and practitioners who have written about effective thaumaturgy; (the art and practice of Magick), such as Isaac Bonewits, Israel Regardie and Aleister Crowley, to name but a very few.

For quick, digestible and effective advice on this subject I will refer you to the author, YouTube tutor and magician, Anassa Rose in her '*10 Most Important Laws for Successful Magick*.' It would be useful to be mindful of law 6, the law of archetypes:

"Who is within is also without. Each magickal practitioner holds a piece of a deity or spirit within them. These spirits and deities are the ones we are most drawn to and work with most often – our Matrons and Patrons."

Final Thoughts

These are not complete Sabbat rituals. There are many examples of these available on the internet at the touch of a button. Rather, these tools can be usefully slotted into any ritual.

Of course I am not breaking any oaths given, regarding the revealing of secrets in the craft, as many similar rituals now populate the web. I am sure that by using and linking with the spiritual energies which abound at these points in the yearly cycle; practitioners will indeed find themselves more connected to the seasons and life in general. So, as well as a straightforward handbook of pagan rituals, the reader practicing these will also find a path to working with the natural development of the self, to energise self-actualisation and beyond.

This work was purposely not overcomplicated with theories or discourse on how magick works, or how a Wiccan circle should be constructed. I assume the reader will have a basic grasp of these concepts.

We at the Circle of Brigid have had a lot of satisfaction and success when using the content that you now have. Aside from real bliss and a feeling of connection to something other, something tangible in nature, which our spiritual and religious sensibilities yearn for, there is a feeling of empowerment. Brigid wants us to feel empowered. She wants us to become illuminated, to take charge of who we are – and finally to return some of that power to nature and the community, engaging with the cycle of being. These Pathworkings will help you attune to who you are as a Wiccan sorcerer. Whether you will develop as a teacher, a healer, a medium for the community, a nature worker, mystic or poet or whatever else – may the light of Brigid illuminate your way; Blessed Be!

Appendix –
A Summary of the Sabbats

Sabbat	Dates	Main aspects/ Symbolism	What the Gods are doing
Imbolc	1st or 2nd February.	Preparing for Spring, a fire festival, but the emphasis is on light rather than fire. The light is returning and strengthening against the darkness of the winter. Here the Goddess is renewed, reborn as the Maid. Lunar light is also seen for inspiration.	A feast for Brigid who brings fertility and the light of the life force back into the world. She is pregnant with the seed (nourished by the Sun) at Yule.
Ostara, The Spring Equinox	20 th, 21 st, 22 cnd, or 23 rd of March.	1st Greater Sabbat or Celtic fire festival (solar festival). The day and night are equal in length. The days will get longer. This is a time of balance and fertility as daffodils, tulips and tree blossoms bloom.	
Beltane	30th April or 1st of May.	The start of the planting cycle. Fertility is celebrated as is fire and light. The warming of the sun continues as its power grows. The phallic symbol of the maypole stands for the reproducing force of nature.	Fire, especially the Bel-fire, the fire of a Celtic God Bel, God of the light with Sun-like qualities.

Sabbat	Dates	Main aspects/ Symbolism	What the Gods are doing
Litha, The Summer Solstice, or Midsummer	20th, 21st, 22nd, or 23rd of June.	2nd Greater Sabbat or Celtic Fire festival (solar festival). Now the longest day and the shortest night of the year. Flowers are being pollinated.	The Sun-God is now at his highest, brightest and his day at its longest, the peak of light and warmth. A battle of powers between light and dark, between the Oak King and the Holly King. The Oak King is the ruler of the year from winter till summer and the Holly King from summer till winter, so the Oak King is defeated by the Holly King on Midsummer.
Lammas or Lughnasadh	1st of August.	The first harvest and some recognition that summer must be coming to an end. A time to harvest ripe berries and grain.	The first harvest festival, named after the Celtic God Lugh. A thanksgiving to the Goddess for her plentiful harvest.

Sabbat	Dates	Main aspects/ Symbolism	What the Gods are doing
Mabon, The Autumn Equinox	20th, 21st, 22nd, or 23rd of September.	3rd Greater Sabbat or Celtic Fire festival (solar festival). The second harvest festival, completion of the harvest. The day and the night are equal in length. Balance and equilibrium are contemplated again. Fermenting wine and beer is typically carried out. A celebration of reaping the benefits of Summer.	Important is the acknowledgement of the waning power of the Sun and the waxing power of the dark.
Samhain	31st October or 1st November.	For many, the Wiccan New Year. A festival of death as leaves fall and life retreats to hibernation. On Samhain is the veil between the worlds the thinnest, so it is possible to contact the spirits of the dead. It is the time of propitiation, divination and communion with the dead.	The dark winter half of the year begins.

Sabbat	Dates	Main aspects/ Symbolism	What the Gods are doing
Yule, The Winter Solstice	20th, 21st, 22nd, or 23rd of December.	4th Greater Sabbat or Celtic Fire festival (solar festival). The longest night and the shortest day of the year but also a promise of a return to the light and life triumphing again. So there is hope and celebration.	The Sun is at its southernmost point in the sky. Celebration of the return of the waxing Sun, rebirth of the Sun-God. Now the Holly King, God of the waning year, is defeated by the Oak King, God of the waxing year. The Goddess who was Death-in-Life at Midsummer is at the moment Life-in-Death, the Queen of the cold darkness is re-fertilized and brings back light and warmth.

References

Editors: A. Dimech, P. Grey & J. Stratton-Kent. (2012). *At the Crossroads* (Limitation 800 standard hardback & 64 hand-bound exemplars – number 613). Publisher: Scarlet Imprint. Pdf Available at:http://dlx.bookzz.org/genesis/880000/bff01eea06eec560dcb7aa15f9526d10/_as/%5BVarious,_Eds._Alkistis_Dimech,_Peter_Grey,_Jake_S(BookZZ.org).pdf

Admin. *The Alchemical Journey* – A Glastonbury Zodiac Mystery School Adventure. (February, 2013). The Alchemy of Imbolc [Online] Available at: http://www.thealchemicaljourney.co.uk/uncategorized/the-alchemy-of-imbolc

Anassa Rose. (18 July 2017). *The 10 Most Important Laws for Successful Magick* Kindle Edition. Publisher: Amazon Media EU S.à r.l.

Bob Chaundy.(Friday, 30 October 2009). *The Burning Times* (BBC NEWS). [online] Available at: http://news.bbc.co.uk/1/hi/magazine/8334055.stm

Brian Bates. (1983). *The Way of Wyrd: The Book of a Sorcerer's Apprentice*. Published by Harper & Row, U.S.A.

Charles Fort. (18 Sept. 2008). *Book of the Damned: The Collected Works of Charles Fort* 2008 (first published in 1919) Publisher: Jeremy P. Tarcher; 1st Jeremy P. Tarcher/Penguin Collected Ed edition.

Charlotte Allen. (Jan 2001 issue). *The Scholars and the Goddess -Historically speaking, the "ancient" rituals of the Goddess movement are almost certainly bunk*, in The Atlantic.com.[online]. Available at: https://www.theatlantic.com/magazine/archive/2001/01/the-scholars-and-the-goddess/305910/

Dennis William Hauck. *The Azoth Ritual.* [online] Available at: http://azothalchemy.org/azoth_ritual.htm

Dennis William Hauck. (1 Apr 2008) *The Complete Idiot's Guide to Alchemy (Complete Idiot's Guides)* 1st Edition, Kindle Edition. Publisher: Alpha; 1 edition.

Doreen Valiente. (1989). *An ABC of Witchcraft: Past and Present.* Publisher: Phoenix Publishing, Incorporated

Doreen Valiente Quotes. *AZ Quotes. [online].* Available at: http://www.azquotes.com/author/18224-Doreen_Valiente

Journal of Shamanism, Spring/Summer 1997, Vol. 10, No. 1 Edith Turner (1997). *The Reality of Spirits.* The Foundation for Shamanic Studies. [online]. Available at: https://www.shamanism.org/articles/article02.html

Journal of the Western Mystery Tradition. No. 3, Vol 1. Autumnal Equinox 2002. *Path-working on the Qabalistic Tree of Life* by Alex Sumner. [online]. Available at: http://www.jwmt.org/v1n3/pathworking.html

Journal of the Western Mystery Tradition. No.6. Vol. 1, Vernal Equinox

2004. Gerald Gardner and the Cauldron of Inspiration: An Investigation into the Source of Gardnarian Witchcraft, Philip Hesetlon. 438 pages. Capall Bann Publishing, 2003. Milverton, Sumerset review by Alex Sumner. [online]. Available at: http://www.jwmt.org/v1n6/gardner.html

Journal of the Western Mystery Tradition No. 10, Vol. 1, Vernal Equinox 2006. Modern Grimoire Magick: Folk Magick and The Solomonic Path. Aaron J. Leitch [online]. Avaliable at: http://jwmt.org/v1n10/modern.html

Michael York. UK. (2009). *The A to Z of New Age Movements*. Publisher: The Scarecrow Press, inc. Lanham. Toronto. Plymouth, pps 142–143

P.E.I Bonewits. (2001). *The Laws of Magic. An Excerpt From Authentic Thaumaturgy* Copyright © 1979, 1998, 2001 c.e., Isaac Bonewits. [online]. Available at: http://www.neopagan. net/AT_Laws.html

Philip Heselton. (22 Feb 2016). Doreen Valiente Witch. Publisher: Centre For Pagan Studies Ltd.

Phil Hine. (Sept 7, 2010). holybooks.com. *Techniques of Modern Shamanism Vol 1–3*.[online]. Available at: https://www. holybooks.com/techniques-of-modern-shamanism-vol-1-3-by-phil-hine/& https://holybooks-lichtenbergpress.netdna-ssl. com/wp-content/uploads/Techniques-of-Modern-Shamanism-vol-2-Walking-Between-The-Worlds.pdf pages: 23–29.

Rodney Orpheus. *A New and Greater Pagan Cult*: Gerald Gardner & Ordo Templi Orientis, [online]. Available at: http://rodneyorpheus.com/writings/occult/a-new-and-greater-pagan-cult-gerald-gardner-ordo-templi-orientis/

Ronald Hutton. (2001). *The Triumph of the Moon*: A History of Modern Pagan Witchcraft. City: Publisher: Oxford University Publishers.

Ronald Hutton (03 Nov 2008) *Modern Pagan Festivals: A Study in the Nature of Tradition, Folklore*, [online]. Available at https://www.tandfonline.com/doi/full/10.1080/00155870802352178

Shri Mataji Nirmala Devi. (2013). *About Sahaja Yoga – Kundalini, Vibrations and Self Realization*. Published online: Vishwa Nirmala Dharma. [online]. Available at: https://www.sahajayoga.org/whatissy/kundalini_self_realization.asp

Susa Morgan Black. *Brigit*. Druidery.org .[online]. Available at: https://www.druidry.org/library/gods-goddesses/brigit

Vivianne Crowley. (Saturday 12th January, 2002). *Carl Jung and the Development of Contemporary Paganism*. Department of Pastoral Studies, Heythrop College, University of London. *Contemporary Religion in Historical Perspective The Development of Paganism: History, Influences and Contexts*, 1880-2002 Conference organised by The Open University Religious Studies Research Group Belief Beyond Boundaries Saturday. [online]. Available at: https://www.academia.edu/9885665/Carl_Jung_and_the_Development_of_Contemporary_Paganism

Images:

Brigid's Cross Image. [online]. Available at: https://www.dreamstime.com/royalty-free-stock-photography-saint-brigid-s-cross-image23113237

Wheel of the Year poster. Wiccan calendar. Vector illustration. [online]. Available at: https://www.123rf.com/photo_75759523_.html

Acknowledgements

Thank yous to: Elizabeth Syson for good advice and initial editing services and authors Dennis William Hauck & Jason Miller for permissions to use their material and quotes.

Lightning Source UK Ltd.
Milton Keynes UK
UKHW022110251119
354217UK00009B/715/P